The School Library Volunteer

Cover photographs by Rod Jolliffe.

THE
SCHOOL LIBRARY
VOLUNTEER

Lillian Biermann Wehmeyer

Illustrations by Lynn Garnica

1975

LIBRARIES UNLIMITED, INC.
Littleton, Colo.

LIBRARIES UNLIMITED, INC.
P.O. Box 263
Littleton, Colorado 80120

Library of Congress Cataloging in Publication Data

Wehmeyer, Lillian Biermann, 1933–
    The school library volunteer.

    Bibliography: p.
    Includes index.
    1. School libraries. 2. Instructional materials
centers. 3. Volunteer workers in libraries. I. Title.
Z675.S3W43   027.8   75-12586
ISBN 0-87287-110-X

TABLE OF CONTENTS

The programmed unit below uses a special paging sequence. The headings and their appropriate problems are shown in the order in which they are to be read in the text. Consequently, pages are not shown in the usual numerical sequence.

The programmed unit below uses a special paging sequence.
The headings and their appropriate problems are shown in the
order in which they are to be read in the text. Consequently,
pages are not shown in the usual numerical sequence.

LIST OF ILLUSTRATIONS

TO THE LIBRARY VOLUNTEER

This book is intended to tell you something about today's multi-media school libraries and how children use them. It also provides information about some of the jobs that you, as a volunteer, will probably be asked to do in your school. Elementary school libraries could not give the level of service that they do without your help. So along with your local school, let us say "thank you" for joining in.

We have written on the assumption that you will be working under the direction of a librarian, for more and more school libraries now have the services of a professional school librarian. However, a section is offered later on for those of you who may be trying to go it alone. More than one school library has been started by determined mothers and finally carried forward by the school district with appropriate paid staff and budget for materials!

Most often you will be asked to do the clerical tasks that take such a big piece out of the librarian's time—time he could put to better use helping children and teachers. These tasks are explained later on. But we shall begin by taking a look at the idea of a multi-media library and the way children best operate within it. Then, when we get to the details of how to do the chores, they will perhaps appear as important as they truly are in the scheme of the total library program.

Maybe you have agreed to help in the library as just one of several ways you might help the school. Or perhaps you particularly like the orderliness of library records or the special feel and smell of new library books. Whatever the reason, you want to know that your time is well spent. So let us pause for a moment to explain why elementary school libraries are worth your effort—although an hour watching youngsters in your own school library will probably do that better than anything we can say.

1 : THE VOLUNTEER
AND THE SCHOOL LIBRARY PROGRAM

WHY A LIBRARY?

Many teachers and parents agree that "a good school program requires the resources and services of a school library," as the American Association of School Librarians declared in 1960. Some research studies have attempted to prove this is so. For example, Mary Virginia Gaver of Rutgers University published a study in 1963 entitled *Effectiveness of Centralized Library Service in Elementary Schools*, which showed some good results after a central school library was established. The difficulty of this research, however, is that it is impossible to separate the school library from many other factors affecting the reading behavior of children. How do we know that it was the library alone that led to these results, and not a new reading program or an enthusiastic new teacher?

So we must admit that our belief in the value of school libraries is more a matter of faith than of proof. However, many other things we do in our schools are also based on faith rather than on scientific proof. We continue to do them because we see that they work, whether or not we have a tool by which we can measure their statistical significance. It is appropriate that schools should gather evidence to prove the value of what they are doing wherever it is possible to do so. But it is also appropriate that we continue to develop programs such as school libraries if we are certain that eventually the evidence will be found.

Although it sounds like starry-eyed romanticism to say so, it is true that a library brings students together with some of the finest teachers, storytellers, artists, and musicians of the past and present. Yes, musicians, too—for today's library usually houses not only books, but also art prints and recordings, film-strips and slides, models and maps. Reading about a painting such as the Mona Lisa is no substitute for seeing it, just as reading cannot convey the sound of Beethoven's *Pastorale Symphony*, or the feel of a bolt that has been tightened firmly but not too much, or the taste of anchovies. Some of these experiences can be stored in a multi-media library in a form other than books.

Educational psychologists tell us that the students who receive these experiences vary, too. Some of them learn better through their ears than their eyes, or from diagrams than from verbal explanations. Or perhaps a child prefers one medium to another simply for the sake of variety. The multi-media library lets the youngster learn about insects from a book, or from a filmstrip or film, or from a study print or transparency.

The multi-media school library provides a wide variety of materials to help children expand their school learning and pursue personal interests. Henry David Thoreau, that lover of nature at Walden Pond, once said that his greatest benefit from Harvard University had been learning to use the library. Today that benefit is available to thousands of elementary school children.

CHILDREN IN THE LIBRARY

Children must feel welcome in the library. The library environment and the people who work there combine to make this happen. Orderly shelves, comfortable furniture, audiovisual (AV) equipment set up, plugged in, and ready for use—and above all an encouraging smile—draw children to return.

Few of today's school libraries limit children to one visit a week with their class group. Some schools have abandoned the class visit completely, although many librarians still find such group visits an opportunity to whet the curiosity of youngsters who might otherwise not come in at all. In either case, children are usually welcome to come and go any time the library is open, as the need arises. Children come individually or in small groups to choose books, to use audiovisual materials, to research a report, or just to explore. The librarian entices them with story hours, book talks, bulletin boards and displays—anything that his imagination can devise. Often volunteers as well as teachers and students offer useful suggestions.

The library must be accessible, if such a program is to succeed. Here volunteers often have an important role. They may keep the library open during the librarian's lunch hour or at times when the librarian must attend meetings elsewhere. In schools where the librarian comes only two or three days a week, it is often the volunteers who make the library available to children on the remaining days.

Students often help to operate the library. They may card and shelve books, make up reading lists for their classmates, decorate bulletin boards, and perform many other tasks. Student helpers must be taught what to do and be supervised as they do it. At times the librarian realizes that it takes almost as much time to supervise them as it would to perform the task himself. But these youngsters are not merely helping the librarian; they are also gaining a sense of participation in and responsibility for the library program, which is more important than the work they do.

For some children the library is a temporary haven; for others it is a doorway to knowledge. In any case, children should find in the library collection material that anticipates their needs, whether that be a pamphlet on how to repair a bicycle, a book of tongue twisters, or a film of a chicken hatching from its egg. Here youngsters can gather information or discover the arts, particularly literature. In the successful multi-media library children will be busy—and usually noisier than we were in the libraries of our childhood.

TEACHERS IN THE LIBRARY

Teachers, too, need to feel welcome in the school library. Most of them, like us, grew up without a school library in their own experience and were not taught how to use the library as a teaching tool in their college training. Librarians, therefore, spend part of their time planning with teachers for improved use of the multimedia facility.

A teacher is responsible for his own class while it is in the library as at any other time. The library staff recognizes this, as do library volunteers. However, a quiet word of reminder or a moment of help to a youngster who needs it is never amiss. Sometimes children from other classes may be in the library at the same time as a class group, and a teacher will not usually give particular attention to those children. His responsibility is to his class, and the role of library staff is to support that responsibility.

THE LIBRARY PROGRAM

There are three thrusts in a school library program, and they are of equal importance: 1) providing information, including the skills of locating materials one is looking for; 2) providing aesthetic experiences through the fine arts, especially literature; 3) helping children develop the social skills and responsibilities required when a learning area is shared with others.

The librarian is something like an orchestra director, emphasizing various aspects of the program in turn, responding to the needs of children, and drawing upon the talents of the entire school staff, the volunteers, and, again, the children. As if that were not enough to occupy his time, the librarian is also responsible for procuring new materials to be used in the program, which requires reading books and previewing audiovisual materials selected from the thousands produced and reviewed each year.

The school library is no longer merely an aid to the classroom program, although it certainly performs that function. And the librarian spends much time planning with teachers, suggesting materials, preparing bibliographies, and presenting lessons that dovetail with classroom instruction. But most children will have a public library available long after they have stopped attending formal schools, and the library program looks forward to that time. The school librarian wants children to discover the many ways in which a library can help them—and wants them to be skillful at using it to the best advantage.

No librarian could possibly find time to do all the activities that are possible within this three-pronged program. We have pointed out that volunteers are often asked to perform routine tasks so that the librarian will be free to use his professional skills in working with children and teachers. But volunteers often can make a valuable contribution to the library program itself, enriching it with their own talents.

Library volunteers can prepare bulletin boards, make up reading lists of good books they have skimmed through themselves, set up displays, and send away for free or inexpensive materials. Volunteers have organized pamphlet and picture files, made tape recordings of picture books, and prepared tape-slide units describing local historical sites, community activities, or the library program itself.

One mother set up a "curiosity corner" each week where something was hidden in a box to be identified by touch, and all the successful guessers had their names posted. Similar ideas could be carried out with math puzzles, descriptions of book characters, or unusual photographs. Volunteers have shared their hobbies with children (with books and magazines available to be checked out when the demonstration was over). Others have led traditional story hours or presented puppet plays based on books. Cooking, sewing, mending, and grooming are topics that mothers have shared with children, presenting library materials with which the youngsters may carry on afterwards. The possibilities are endless. Your librarian will be happy to learn of any talents you are willing to share.

HELPING CHILDREN IN THE LIBRARY

Sometimes there are more children asking for help than the librarian can possibly get to. At such times a library volunteer can step in and assist with some of the requests.

Everyone who works in a library should know how to operate the audio-visual equipment that is set out at listening-viewing stations for children to use. It is best to have the AV equipment set up and ready for the children before they arrive. There should be a listening-viewing station for each medium housed in the library. If there are filmstrips in the library, for example, there should be a filmstrip viewer. If there are sound filmstrips with the narration on cassettes, one listening-viewing station must provide a combination filmstrip-cassette machine, or a cassette player and separate filmstrip viewer side by side. Equipment will last longer if it need not be moved to accommodate any such combination media.

Not only can volunteers show children how to use equipment and materials properly, but they can keep a weather eye out for youngsters who may be tempted to play with equipment, rather than to use it. If a phonograph record can be heard even though a listening post is plugged into the machine, the player is turned up too loud. If children are switching the speed frequently on a tape recorder, they are probably playing with the effects of doubling and halving the speed. If a headset is plugged into the microphone input on a tape machine, the student may well be experimenting with recording, at the same time erasing the original material (recently manufacturers have begun to provide players-only for use in multi-media libraries to avoid just such problems).

Library volunteers should also know something about using a card catalog and magazine index to locate library materials. A good way to brush up your skills in this area is to read a book for children on the subject; not only will you be able to get through it quickly, but the examples given will be similar to the questions children will ask. A good title is *The Children's Book on How to Use Books and Libraries* by Carolyn Mott and Leo B. Baisden (3rd. ed.; New York, Scribner's, 1968).

Often a child knows how to use library indexes, but he is not looking up a term that is used in the card catalog, magazine index, or other index. Cross references are not always as complete as we might like, partly due to lack of time

Cooking Up a Library Program

and partly because children sometimes use terms that indexers do not think of. For the card catalog, your library may have a copy of *Sears List of Subject Headings*, which lists most topics, other than proper names, that you might be looking for. In this list, the words in dark, boldface type are the ones used in the card catalog. The index section at the back of *Children's Catalog* from H. W. Wilson Co. is also liberally supplied with cross-references.

A children's book that deals with problems in finding the appropriate key word to look up is *The First Book of Facts and How to Find Them* by David C. Whitney (New York, Franklin Watts, 1966). A library volunteer will find it well worth the time it takes to read this short book, again because the examples are much like the questions children will bring to the library.

Whenever time permits, the process of helping children can be made into a teaching situation. If you explain what you are doing as you go along, the youngster has a better idea of how to proceed the next time he needs information. If you ask the child to show you how to load a piece of audiovisual equipment after your demonstration, he is more likely to remember how it is done. It is indeed tempting to short-circuit the catalogs and indexes and take the student directly to what he needs, if you happen to remember where it is, but that teaches him only to depend on an adult the next time. On the other hand, if as many children as possible find their own materials on most occasions, more time is available to help those youngsters who are not finding what they need on their own. As we help children, we show them how to help themselves.

If you wear a name tag while you are on duty, some children may feel a bit braver about asking for your help. And a friendly smile can reassure a youngster that you are there if he needs you, even as you hold back from smothering him with unnecessary assistance.

READING CHILDREN'S BOOKS

If you want to be especially valuable to the library staff and teachers of your school, you will want to check out a book or two yourself and read it. When you are able to tell just enough about a book to interest a child in reading it, you will find yourself sought after in the library. But where to begin?

You might set out first to read the titles suggested in any of the several books listed below. Or any new books that come in and attract your interest. Or the books that are really popular with the students at your school. Or perhaps the books that are well written but less popular—the "best sellers" do not need any help to find an audience!

Standards of quality in children's books need not be compromised to find interesting and exciting titles these days. And in your search for the good ones you may, if you are a parent or grandparent, find some suggestions you can pass along to children in your own family. Here are a few suggested lists from which to choose:

Arbuthnot, May Hill, ed. *Children's Books Too Good to Miss*. 6th ed. (Cleveland, Press of Case Western Reserve University, 1971).

Arbuthnot, May Hill. *Children's Reading in the Home.* (Glenview, Ill., Scott Foresman, 1969).

Gillespie, John, and Diana Lembo. *Introducing Books: A Guide for the Middle Grades.* (New York, R. R. Bowker, 1970).

Larrick, Nancy. *A Parent's Guide to Children's Reading.* Rev. and enl. 3rd ed. (New York, Pocket Books, 1969).

National Congress of Parents and Teachers and Children's Services Division, American Library Association. *Let's Read Together: Books for Family Enjoyment.* 3rd ed. (Chicago, American Library Association, 1969).

National Council of Teachers of English. *Adventuring with Books.* 2nd ed. (New York, Citation Press, 1973).

RULES AND REGULATIONS

When library volunteers meet at a workshop, it is not long before the question of discipline arises. The multi-media library is a busy place. Quiet study and absorbing discussions, library skills instruction, book talks and storytelling, listening and viewing of audiovisual materials—all may happen at the same time. Rarely is a school library large enough to accommodate these conflicting needs. Consequently, one can rarely hear a pin drop, or even a hammer!

The librarian sets the tone for library discipline. Volunteers and other library staff members work within that framework. Some flexibility is necessary; some class groups, for instance, seem always to be comparatively noisy and others amazingly quiet. But there will be a maximum noise level that the librarian will accept, and you will soon develop a feel for what that level is.

There are really only two basic rules for library behavior. The first is: *be considerate of the needs of other library users—including the people who work there.* The second is implied in the first but worth stating because it is so important in the library setting: *be careful in handling library materials and equipment.* Even young children can remember two rules. In most libraries the librarian will appreciate your quietly reminding a youngster about either of these rules. Indeed, children can be encouraged to remind one another. The library is a place to be shared, and everyone who shares it must work together to keep it running smoothly. See page 9 for a chart of the two basic library rules.

Should you happen to be alone in the library at a moment when a conflict has arisen about use of materials or equipment, or any other matter, think of the "law of marginal antisepsis." This principle suggests that when children's needs conflict, one should look for a solution that will help one group or individual and that will at least not hurt the other. For example, if two youngsters need the only available filmstrip viewer at the same time, perhaps you can determine that one of them is preparing a report for the same afternoon while the other is pursuing a personal interest. Then perhaps the second child can be persuaded to return later in the day to use the machine. This "law" is explained in *When We Deal with Children* by Fritz Redl (New York, Free Press, 1966).

Children who are in the multi-media library should have a library purpose. The purpose may be very specific, such as gathering information for a report on the

Sioux Indians, or rather vague, such as finding a good book to read. But children whose behavior suggests they need a spot for social conversation or for lively games may certainly be asked to postpone those activities or to leave the room. (If the teacher is in the room with the children, they may be referred to him, of course.)

If children are asked to leave the library during class time, your school may require that the teacher be notified. During recess or lunch hour, of course, the playground or another recreational area is probably available for the children. In either case, however, it is essential that the children understand that you have asked them to leave only because their behavior at the moment is inappropriate to the library setting. Certainly they will be welcome to return when they have a library purpose to pursue.

Recurring behavior problems should be brought to the attention of the librarian, who may occasionally banish the youngster from the library for the rest of the day, or even the rest of the week. However, he will always work on the assumption that by the child's next visit he will have grown just a bit more and will probably manage things better.

A positive approach to discipline is essential. Children are growing and learning; they may do better on another occasion. Equally important, a youngster who has demonstrated consideration for others or responsibility in handling materials and equipment certainly deserves a word of approval. Our goal must be to encourage children to take responsibility for self-discipline wherever they may be.

OVERDUE MATERIALS

After questions about discipline in the school library comes the issue of handling overdue materials. Volunteers often write up overdue lists or notices; later in this book we shall deal with the clerical routines involved. However, the chore of dealing with overdue notices (and with the children who receive them) will be less annoying if the task is seen as an opportunity to teach children about their responsibilities in the matter. Again, we assume that the child is growing, that he will learn to carry out this responsibility given time and practice.

Occasionally a youngster with overdue library materials is criticized to such an extent that he decides not to check out any more books. This is not, of course, our intention. Often the best readers lose track of something they have checked out, so the youngster on the overdue list may be an eager library user whose enthusiasm we wish to encourage. (For this reason, many school libraries have abandoned the practice of charging fines.) On the other hand, children need to accept responsibility for returning library materials on time so that other students may use them, and so that library staff need not spend valuable time reminding the tardy ones.

Library volunteers should mention to the librarian those youngsters who have overdue materials time and time again, especially if several items are involved. For these repeaters the library staff may use one or more of the procedures suggested on page 10. Note that each step is intended to help the youngster begin to take the responsibility for prompt returns on his own.

Library Rules Poster

Initially, children may be encouraged to return materials just as soon as they have finished with them, for youngsters sometimes think they should not return materials until the date due. The librarian may suggest to the child that he find a particular place at school and at home where he will keep his library materials, so that they will not be lost among other things. The child should understand, too, how much time someone must take to send overdue notices to him; helping write notices for a half hour or so may make this point.

The pupil's name may continue to appear on the overdue list despite these efforts. In that case the child may commit himself to a limit of one or two books at a time. He must understand that the librarian is not enforcing this rule (for there is no way that can be done), but that it is his responsibility to do so. The next time that his name appears on the overdue list with more than the agreed-upon number of items outstanding, however, firmer measures may be in order.

Now the child may set up a borrower's card which he keeps in the library. Each item he checks out is listed, and later crossed off when returned. Either of these limitations is undertaken, however, with the understanding that it is only temporary, until the child has shown that he no longer needs it.

Incidentally, a blanket rule that limits the number of books a child can take is impractical in an open library situation where children come and go all day long. A librarian or teacher may encourage children to limit themselves in the lower grades. But to announce a "rule" may result in children discovering that rules can be broken. There is no way that the library staff can be sure that a particular child has obeyed the rule unless he happens to keep more than the stated number of items overdue. Never announce a firm rule unless it can be enforced. In this case it is certainly more important that children are able to visit the library often than that a strict limit be imposed on the number of items they can check out. As a librarian once remarked, a library program would be totally successful if the shelves were empty every night and full the next morning.

Children need approval for good library citizenship. The notice on page 11 is used in one district when materials which have been missing for several weeks are returned to the library.

THE LIBRARY CHAIRMAN

When community volunteers are helping the librarian in the school library, much time can be taken up with recruiting people, arranging for substitutes, and communicating with volunteers on a variety of details. A library chairman will relieve the librarian of much of this detail, so that the volunteer program will not take much of the librarian's time. The chairman can make telephone calls, transmit information, remind volunteers who may have forgotten their scheduled time, and sometimes assist in training new people. The chairman may also arrange a tea to recruit new volunteers, or to say "thank you" to those who have been helpers for the year.

The library chairman will need ingenuity and determination in recruiting volunteers. Telephone calls, written notices carried home by children, mothers' teas—all are occasions for recruiting help. There are many tasks to be done in the

Lost Materials Notice

THE LOST

HAS BEEN FOUND!!!

The following material, which had been checked out

by _____ was returned to
the library today. Thank you!

_____

_____

                                    Library

library. Some require a regular time slot of two or three hours each week. Others need to be done only when a new shipment of materials has arrived, or when a due date has just passed, or when some other occasional job has come up. Some require working with children and teachers; others are clerical tasks, to be done in a work room or quiet corner. When recruiting library volunteers, it is a good idea to list several different tasks, and indicate the time requirements and special skills (such as typing or knowledge of AV equipment) that are necessary. Volunteers vary in their interests, so careful description of each task may result in a greater number of volunteers.

Another of the library chairman's tasks involves substitutes. Volunteers who cannot keep their regular time should have a list of substitutes to contact, or should contact the library chairman, who may be responsible for getting substitutes whenever needed. Library staff and teachers depend on their volunteers, and sometimes it is essential to use a substitute.

The library chairman should be a person who thinks the multi-media library is important. The chairman is a key person in the success of the volunteer program.

BOOK FAIRS

Volunteers are often asked to organize a book fair for the school. The primary purpose of a book fair is to get quality children's books into the homes of the community. Making money to buy new library materials is only a secondary consideration.

Much advance planning is necessary if a book fair is to be successful. A cooperative book dealer must be found. Sometimes retail stores will allow a discount for school book fairs; in other cases wholesale outlets will be willing to cooperate. In recent years it has become more difficult for book dealers to make ends meet, so finding a cooperative firm may be the most difficult step.

The Children's Book Council in New York has published a pamphlet, "Planning a School Book Fair," which includes many helpful suggestions.

WITHOUT A LIBRARIAN

In many schools, community volunteers, especially mothers, have started library programs that were eventually taken up by the school or district and carried forward with appropriate staff and budget for materials. Such an approach can be a good beginning.

If the principal can find a room, or perhaps even a closet, or a wall in a hallway or multi-purpose room where books and audiovisual materials can be organized, a small library collection can be gathered. From the beginning, only materials of good quality should be placed in the collection. Standard lists are available from the American Library Association, the H. W. Wilson Co., and the Bro-Dart Foundation. (See page 119, "Sources and Resources.")

Volunteers cannot classify and catalog materials (unless there happens to be a retired librarian in the group), but cataloging services are now available from several firms. Some companies provide catalog cards only, others catalog cards plus checkout card and pocket; some will even paste the pocket inside, label the call number on the spine of the materials or AV box, and provide suitable plastic covers or other containers. Since the companies that provide this service are constantly changing, they are not listed here, but a library advisor can suggest several for your consideration (such an advisor can usually be found in your county or state department of education). Failing that, the school librarian in a neighboring district, or the nearest public librarian, should be able to give you advice in getting started.

Once the library has been set up, the information in Chapter 2 of this book will help you with the clerical procedures. Further reading in books and such magazines as *School Library Journal* and *School Media Quarterly* will help you along your way. Your library advisor or the American Association of School Librarians in Chicago can suggest resource materials.

If the program is to be a success, it must have the support of the school principal and faculty. A committee of parents who are interested and willing to work can probably win that support.

A FEW LAST SUGGESTIONS

One of the most difficult tasks in a volunteer program is keeping everybody in touch with everybody else. To help solve this problem, the Los Altos School

District (California) suggests keeping a library log at the library desk. Here all library staff, from students to the district librarian, write questions, comments, suggestions, and announcements. Whenever a volunteer comes to work in the library, he is responsible for reading all entries since his last visit.

Paid library staff members sometimes find it awkward to tell a volunteer that they do not have time for conversation. The library staff people know how much they need the help of the volunteers, and they do not want to do anything that might make the volunteer feel unwelcome. So a volunteer can be very helpful by remembering to keep social conversation to a minimum.

Volunteers, like the regular staff members, are expected to provide a model for children. If children are expected to keep voices down and restrict conversation, so must the adults. If children may not bring food or drinks into the library, neither should the adults who work there. Youngsters will often imitate the behavior they see around them.

Volunteers may want to check into the school policy on use of the staff room or other faculty facilities, and they should investigate the appropriate procedures for purchasing supplies (such as display materials) before doing so; often the school can obtain a discount on materials the volunteer may need. Any accidents to children, adults, or oneself should be reported promptly to the librarian. And finally, it is usually poor practice to carry any large sum of money or other valuables, or to leave a purse out in the open in a school.

By thinking in advance of possible problem areas, the volunteer can ask questions and help keep things running smoothly.

A SPECIAL REQUEST

Having considered the purpose of the multi-media library program and some aspects of its operation, we are about ready to turn our attention to specific procedures that you, as a volunteer, will probably be asked to carry out. Before doing so, however, let us pause to consider a problem that has sometimes arisen when community volunteers participate in the school program.

Volunteers in schools sometimes learn information about children or staff members that should be kept confidential. When you become a volunteer, you should assume that same professional respect for such information as is demanded of teachers and other staff members. Personal information should stay within the walls of the school.

Volunteers may at times observe incidents among children or between teachers and children that appear less than ideal. Here, the volunteer should keep in mind that the incident is but one in an entire pattern of relationships, and that the incident may well be appropriate within that pattern. Moreover, teachers and children in school are as subject to occasional error as anyone else. The volunteer who is genuinely concerned about something he has witnessed or heard about should consult with the teacher, librarian, or other appropriate staff member, rather than risk sharing an inaccurate or unjust impression with members of the community.

In many cases, on the other hand, volunteers see genuine needs within the library program or the school as a whole, and can give honest and wholehearted support to requests for funds or other staff efforts to improve the school. Such support is genuinely appreciated by school personnel who are trying to do the best possible job for the children of the community.

2 : THE VOLUNTEER
AND SCHOOL LIBRARY ROUTINES

VOLUNTEERS AT WORK

Earlier we discussed some of the creative ways in which volunteers assist school library programs. However, much of a volunteer's time is often spent in clerical tasks, so that the library staff will have more time to spend assisting children and teachers. Many of these routines are described in the following pages.

Some librarians prepare a checklist in advance, so that even if the volunteer arrives while the librarian is making a presentation to a class group, the volunteer will know immediately what needs to be done. An example of such a checklist is shown below.

Library task assignment for _____

Date _____

Please perform these tasks in the sequence indicated:

_____   Card returned books (be sure copy number matches).
_____   Shelve books which have cards in them (verify the card just
          before you shelve the book).
_____   Straighten shelves beginning at _____. Write
          here the call number at which you leave off _____.
_____   Read shelves beginning at _____. Write here
          the call number at which you leave off _____.
_____   Write notices for blue-card materials:
          _____First notices   _____Second notices
          _____Third notices
_____   Write notices for overdue white-card materials:
          _____First notices   _____Second notices
          _____Third notices
_____   File checkout cards in circulation file.

(continued on next page)

_____	File these catalog cards in the card catalog.
_____	Count these cards for inventory.
_____	File these cards in the shelf list file.
_____	Check in new materials:
	_____Unpack _____Stamp school name
	_____File teachers' manuals
	_____Add duplicate copies to shelf list and count for inventory.
_____	Stamp and shelve magazines
_____	Check reserves:
	_____Locate new reserves _____Send out pickup notices
_____	Do new bulletin board.
_____	Set up display in display case.
_____	Type book orders.
_____	Check in textbooks, count, and add to inventory.
_____	Work on shelf inventory.
_____	Pull catalog cards.

We shall begin with the "circulation system," the procedures by which materials are checked out of the library, returned and checked back in, and returned to their proper location on the library shelves.

CHECKING IN MATERIALS

One of the easier tasks for the beginning volunteer is to check materials back into the library. The first step is to "card" or "slip" the book or media item. This means to find the checkout card and replace it in the pocket of the item.

The cards for materials that have been checked out are kept in the "circulation file." Cards for student materials are filed according to the due date, and then alphabetically by author. Sometimes non-fiction (numbered) items are filed by the call number, while only fiction and easy books are in order by author. The proper card must be found for each returned item.

Some libraries still use the accession number, which is different for each item. Most libraries today, however, use copy numbers. In this case, the checkout card must be matched to the pocket for author, title, *and* copy number. Since some books have very similar titles, this matching must be carefully done (see page 17 for an illustration that demonstrates matching the checkout card to the pocket).

Before you put the card into its pocket, check to be sure that there is still space for the next student to sign his name. If not, a new card should be typed before the item is put back on the shelf. Some libraries show that this is "card 2" or "card 3" for the book as an indication of its popularity. Ask your librarian about this.

Some libraries cross off the last borrower's name when the book is carded. If you do this, cross through with just a single line so that the name can still be read. Occasionally errors will happen!

Carding Books

To verify that a checkout card is the correct one for a book, match these four items on the card and pocket—call number, author, title, and copy number.

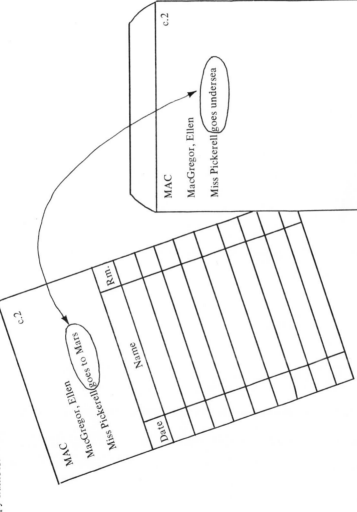

MAC
MacGregor, Ellen
Miss Pickerell goes to Mars

c.2

Name   Rm.

Date

MAC
MacGregor, Ellen
Miss Pickerell goes undersea

c.2

The checkout card and book pocket shown above do not match because the titles are different.

Check-in time is also your opportunity to inspect materials for damage, such as crayon marks in books or magazines, missing parts in audiovisual sets, scratched records, torn recording tape or film. Any damage should be brought to the librarian's attention. A child's parents may be expected to pay for items that need to be replaced. Volunteers may be able to repair some of the damaged items.

Sometimes you may not be able to find the checkout card. Almost every library has a shelf marked "Snags" or "Strays" for just such books. One does not simply type a new card, for somewhere in the file may be the original card, with some child's name on it. Or another copy of the book may be on the shelf with this copy's card in it. The entire file should be searched before a new card is typed. Usually the librarian waits a week or two, then searches the file and shelves, and only then types a new card. The new card is marked to show that it is a duplicate. Also, at the front of the circulation file a list is kept of duplicate cards that have been typed during that school year, so that a student is not accidentally charged for a book that has since been checked out again on a duplicate card.

Duplicate Checkout Card

```
MAC                                    c.1

MacGregor, Ellen

Miss Pickerell goes to Mars

        dup 10/74
```

List of Duplicate Checkout Cards

```
            1974-75 dups

595.7-L A wasp is born c.2
MAC MacGregor-Miss Pickerell
goes to Mars c.1
```

Many schools keep teachers' checkout cards in a separate part of the file, because teachers often keep books for a longer checkout time. You will want to remember to look there for cards you cannot find.

SHELVING MATERIALS

After materials have been carded, they are ready to be returned to the shelves. Just before an item is shelved, however, check to be sure that the card and the pocket match. This is not only to catch any errors, but also because smaller children sometimes return their books to the shelving cart instead of to the proper return area. This checking step is sometimes called "verifying" (see page 17).

Various materials may be shelved in different parts of the library. Easy books for younger children are often separate from fiction, and both are always separate from non-fiction. Other materials that are often kept in separate locations are reference materials, magazines, pamphlets, and, sometimes, short story collections.

Audiovisual materials may be shelved with books whenever their size permits; this is called "integrated shelving." The advantage of this system is that children can find all the materials about, say, insects in one place. Firms that specialize in library supplies are now providing sturdy cardboard containers in a variety of sizes and shapes so that audiovisual materials may be placed on bookshelves. However, many libraries have too little space to allow for integrated shelving. In this case, audiovisual materials must often be placed in cabinets and drawers built to accommodate them. Since such cabinets and drawers do not provide space for checkout cards, the cards must be kept in a file, usually at the checkout desk.

On pages 38 to 62 is a self-instructional unit you can use to teach yourself how to arrange materials in order for shelving. Follow the instructions carefully.

STRAIGHTENING SHELVES

Shelves are straightened frequently so that all the materials in the library look neat. When straightening shelves, you pay little attention to correct shelf order of materials—although, of course, if you notice that something is far from its correct location, you should put it where it belongs.

An average-sized elementary school library of a few thousand volumes can be straightened in about half an hour, using the method described here. Shelves should be straightened once a day, so that students will have the impression of an orderly environment when they come to the multi-media library room.

Shelves will look neat if everything is lined up with the front edge of the shelf. To do this quickly, follow the procedure outlined on page 20. When the shelf has been lined up as shown, slide the bookend loosely into place. If you squeeze the materials tightly to the left, they will slide over as soon as someone removes an item from the shelf. Materials should be standing erect, but not packed together.

Straightening Shelves

Take 1/3 to 1/2 of the materials on the shelf between your hands. Press your hands toward each other, and pull the material forward so that everything is hanging slightly over the front edge of the shelf.

Use the flat of your hand to line up the materials with the front edge of the shelf.

This task requires a bit of energy, but the result will often be a neater, and sometimes even quieter, library room. Children will be more likely to leave things in good order if they find them that way.

READING SHELVES

Reading shelves is a far more time-consuming task than straightening shelves. In this procedure, each item on the shelves is checked, one by one, to see that everything is in precisely the right place according to call number.

The librarian may ask you to continue from the spot where the last volunteer left off; in this way the entire library can usually be "read" once or twice a month. Sometimes very popular sections will get an extra reading between the complete circuits.

If your library shelves do not fit tightly against the wall, but instead have a small space at the back, then things may fall down behind. Shelf-reading time is also an opportunity to look behind things on the bottom shelf to see whether any materials have become "lost" there.

This may also be the time to do some "shifting." If the library shelves are extremely crowded, it may be necessary to move some books from tightly packed shelves to some that are partly empty. Since materials must stay in proper order, however, it may be necessary to make adjustments over the space of several shelves. When doing this, remember that materials must be arranged from shelf to shelf and from section to section as shown on page 42.

REPAIRING MATERIALS

Even with the most careful of library users, materials sometimes become damaged. Minor book repairs are often done by volunteers, using one of the repair manuals provided by library supply houses (Demco, Gaylord, etc.). Often these manuals are free. Sometimes these companies will provide a free workshop in repair techniques, to demonstrate the use of their products.

Torn pages should always be mended with "Magic Mending Tape." Ordinary "Scotch" transparent tape becomes brittle and eventually falls off, leaving a yellow, sticky residue. Also, some glues are especially prepared for use on objects that must bend.

On the other hand, special library mending supplies are expensive. Sometimes it may be better economy to send a book to the bindery, or even to buy a new copy, than to use a large amount of repair material and time trying to save it.

Repair materials are available also for audiovisual materials—filmstrips, tape recordings, and motion picture film in particular. Since AV materials cannot be rebound and often cost more than books, somewhat more time and material may be justified in repairing them.

CHECKING OUT MATERIALS

When students or teachers check out materials, it is essential that the library have a record of what has been taken, and that the borrower know when the item is due to be returned. In most school libraries, the borrower signs a checkout card, which lists the call number, author, title, and copy number of the item being taken. The date due is stamped on a slip in the book, or a pre-stamped date due slip is inserted in the pocket of the item being taken. Volunteers frequently are asked to supervise the checkout desk to be sure that students write their names legibly and that the date due is properly indicated in the item being checked out.

In a variation on the above practice, the pre-stamped date due slips (page 22) are available in a box on top of the desk. A borrower signs the checkout card, drops it into a box on the checkout desk, and takes the appropriate pre-stamped date due slip himself. The advantage of this system is that a student can check out the book he wants, leaving the library staff member or volunteer free to help other students in the library. From time to time, however, the checkout desk should be supervised; students need to be reminded that the checkout process is very important and that it must be correctly done.

Pre-stamped date due slips may be used over and over until all the stamping area has been filled. As can be seen on page 22, a date due slip for overnight materials need not have the date stamped on it but can simply be re-used. If checkout cards for overnight materials, such as encyclopedias, are a different color from the usual checkout cards, the overnight date due slip should be of a matching color.

Pre-Stamped Date Due Slip

```
            DATE DUE

Oct 1 75
  NOV 1 75
```

Overnight Date Due Slip

```
            DATE DUE

Blue-card materials are due
before 9 a.m. the very next
school day.
```

Teachers usually want to keep materials for longer than the normal checkout periods. A special date due slip (a teacher's circulation slip) may be used (see below). Actually, the slip does not show a date due at all, but provides a place for the teacher to sign his name. This is helpful because teacher checkouts are usually filed by the teacher's name or room number. To save the teacher's time, some libraries refile the teacher circulation slips, already signed, with the checkout cards in the teacher's checkout file. Then, when the teacher takes out more materials, he can use the circulation slips that already bear his name.

Teacher's Circulation Slip

TEACHER'S CIRCULATION SLIP

Please sign your name so we can
card this item promptly when you
return it. Thank you!

Mrs. Johnson _Room 34_

Pamphlets and magazines are checked out in many libraries. They usually do not have typed checkout cards. Rather, forms may be used as shown on page 25. It is helpful to have the pamphlets or magazines put into a numbered envelope. If no two envelopes carry the same number, it is much easier to find the correct checkout slip for materials when they are returned. The envelope can carry the instructions that the material is to be returned the next day, or a pocket may be pasted on to hold one of the pre-stamped date due slips.

The checkout system described here, with the possibility of self-checkout when library workers are busy, has proved especially valuable in school libraries that must be kept open part of the time by volunteers. Students do not waste time waiting for someone to come and date stamp their materials, no matter how busy the library happens to be at that moment, and library staff can keep an eye on the

MAGAZINE and PAMPHLET CHECKOUT

* TAKE AN ENVELOPE BIG ENOUGH TO HOLD THE MAGAZINES OR PAMPHLETS –

* FILL IN ONE OF THE BLUE SLIPS –

← magazines, pamphlets →

* PUT THE SLIP IN THE CHECKOUT BOX–

Magazine Checkout Form

	ENVELOPE NUMBER **6**
	Month/Day/Year on Magazine
Title of Magazine	
Popular Science	*Oct. 1974*
Ranger Rick's	*Jan. 1975*
Name *John Marsh*	Room No. *3*
Date Due *June 6, '75*	

Pamphlet Checkout Form

PAMPHLET(S)

Envelope No. _____ *4* _____

How Many?	Subject
3	*Africa*
2	*Animals*

Name *Cynthia Smart*
Room No. *4*
Date Due *Oct. 4, '75*

Book and AV Checkout Poster

BOOK and A-V CHECKOUT

* WRITE YOUR FULL NAME AND ROOM NUMBER ON THE BLUE or white CHECKOUT CARD —

* PUT THE CHECKOUT CARD IN THE BOX —

* TAKE A DATE-DUE SLIP —

← *white* or *blue* →

FOR THE POCKET OF THE BOOK OR THE A-V ITEM.

checkout desk from across the room, while still helping other children or teachers find material or operate equipment.

The usual loan period for materials (other than reference books and audio-visual items) in a school library is one week. The date stamp or pre-stamped date due slips must be changed each morning. It is important to remember that the date due must not fall on a holiday.

Some schools have tried a twice-a-month date due, with books falling due on the school day nearest to the 1st and 15th of each month. This simplifies the filing system and makes it easier to find checkout cards when materials are returned. With this system, the date due is changed on the 8th and 20th of the month, and the loan period varies from one to three weeks. For example:

> books checked out from January 8 to January 19 are due February 1;
> books checked out from January 20 to February 7 are due February 15.

The only difficulty with this system has been that some children lose track of materials if they are not due for three weeks.

As much as possible, all the materials in the media center should be checked out with one simple procedure. This makes it much easier for children to remember what they must do. As a final note, no matter how eloquently a child or teacher insists that he will return an item in "just a few minutes," every item that leaves the room should always be properly charged out to the person who is borrowing it.

THE CIRCULATION FILE

At the end of each school day, or first thing the following morning, the checkout cards must be filed. This file is called the circulation file. A teacher's checkout cards are usually filed behind his name or room number. Student checkout cards are filed behind the date due, and then alphabetically by author. Some libraries file non-fiction cards by the Dewey Decimal number, in the same order described in the teach-yourself unit on shelving (Chapter 3).

Before the cards are filed, each one must be stamped with the date due or the date taken out, as the librarian prefers. Some libraries also keep a daily or occasional count of the number of items checked out. Find out whether your library does this before you file the cards.

OVERDUE NOTICES

A day or so after materials have come overdue, notices are usually written. Sometimes a list is made for each classroom. This usually requires "unfiling" and refiling the checkout file, so individual notices are often preferred. Usually two notices—and sometimes more—are written before the parents are notified.

Checkout Reminder Poster

Each notice that is sent should be recorded on the checkout card just under the student's name. A handwritten date is usually enough to show that the notice has been sent.

Cardboard markers reading "First notice" and "Second notice" can be purchased from a library supply house or can be made locally. If such a marker is inserted in the circulation file just behind the last card for which that kind of notice has been written, the next volunteer will know where to begin. See page 30 for examples of a "Second notice" and "Third notice."

Many schools hold parents responsible for paying for lost library materials. For this purpose, a bill is sent to the parents, often not until the end of the school year. A volunteer should always check with the librarian or school principal before mailing any bills, since most schools have one or more families who are in difficult circumstances and will not be expected to pay.

Parents often appreciate knowing that library items are missing before the end of the school year, so that they can help the student look for whatever is lost. A form for such a letter is suggested as the third notice in the sequence illustrated on page 30.

First Notice–Overdue Library Item Reminder

Name   Room

Have you forgotten something?
Please return this book
to the school library.

Author

Title

Copy No.

Date Due

LAFAYETTE SCHOOL DISTRICT

Second Notice—Overdue Library Item Reminder

Name _____ Room _____

OH DEAR! THIS IS YOUR
SECOND REMINDER!
The following library
material is overdue:

CALL NO. _____
AUTHOR _____
TITLE _____
COPY NO. _____
DATE DUE _____

Please come in right away!
The next notice will go to your home!

Third Notice—Overdue Library Item Reminder

To the Parents of

_____

Good library users forget to return materials on time occasionally. Your youngster has not returned the item(s) listed below. We will continue to look for this material here at school, but we thought that perhaps if we contacted you now, while the material might still be fresh in your mind, you would be able to help your child find the mislaid item. Thank you.

_____

_____

(Signed) _____

Overdue notices have sometimes been handled in such a way that the experience was unnecessarily harsh for the children involved. Some suggestions for a constructive approach to the overdue problem have been outlined in the first part of this book.

RECEIVING NEW MATERIALS

This book does not include detailed instructions for processing library materials. Several manuals are available on the subject. Moreover, the details vary from school to school; each library or district should prepare its own specific directions if volunteers are to help with the processing of materials. Furthermore, we hope that there is a central processing center in your district or county, or that the district makes use of a commercial processor.

Even when materials arrive "ready for the shelf," however, there are usually several steps that must be attended to. If the materials come directly from a commercial firm, items must be carefully checked against orders. When time permits, it is also a good idea to check for faulty bindings, pages that are missing or that have been bound upside down, or other flaws. It is much easier to exchange materials if errors are discovered promptly.

There will sometimes be a note that a teacher has requested a particular item; such items should be set aside as they are checked in, since the librarian will want to notify the teacher that the order has arrived. Be sure you understand how to check off materials as they come in, and where to put the order slips, packing lists, and copies of purchase orders.

Books should be opened properly. Hold the book on a flat surface, spine down. Fold back the front cover and the first several pages; then run your hand down the center where the pages come together, pressing downward as you do so. Repeat the procedure at the back of the book. Keep folding down ten or so pages from the front and then the back, running your hand down so that the pages lie flat on the cover, until you get to the center of the book. This will help prevent cracking the glue or breaking the stitches that hold the book together.

Items then need to be identified with the school name and address. The easiest way to do this is to use a rubber stamp; stamp the name on the pocket, on the title page, and perhaps at one or two more locations in the book.

Each item must also have a copy number. If you are dealing with a commercial processing firm, you will need to assign a copy number to every item, and then to record this information on the shelf list card. If items come from a district processing center, this may be done for you, or perhaps only duplicate copies will need to have a copy number entered on the checkout card, pocket, and shelf list card. Be sure to ask the librarian if you have any questions as you assign copy numbers.

No two copies of the same item ever get the same copy number, even if you know that the previous copy was destroyed. Each copy must be listed on the shelf list card.

A shelf list card and a set of catalog cards usually come in the pocket of the library item. They must be removed before the items are shelved into the collection. Call numbers and catalog cards should never be changed without checking with the librarian; some standard library cataloging rules may look peculiar until you have learned the reasons for their use.

THE SHELF LIST

The shelf list is one of the most important records in the library. It is a complete inventory file of every item in the library collection. It is kept in the same order as the materials on the shelves. That is, cards in the shelf list are filed exactly as described in the self-teaching unit on shelving library materials.

Always check with the librarian before you file cards into the shelf list. Some librarians type up a list of new materials to post for the information of students and teachers. Usually, some sort of inventory count is maintained of the number of items of each type in the library collection, and this is usually done from the shelf list cards just before they are filed.

A shelf list card looks much like the main entry card in the card catalog, except that it shows the exact number of copies of an item in the collection and what happened to previous copies. The date the item was purchased and the original price are often shown, too.

Shelf List Card

```
940.53    Lord, Walter
L            A night to remember. Holt, 1955.
             209p. illus.

c.1  9/56  Missing in inventory 6/72
c.2 11/72  $ 4.50



          1. Titanic (Steamship)  I. Title
```

RESERVES

Many school libraries have only one or two copies of an item, even though it may be very popular. Therefore, children may request an item that has been checked out, asking that it be held for them. This is called placing a reserve.

When a student has placed a reserve, you may be asked to mark the checkout card in the circulation file so that the book will be set aside when it is returned. The first step is to check the shelf to be sure the item is out; sometimes children miss the item they are looking for. The next step is to check the shelf list to see how many copies are in the library collection. Finally, you will search through the circulation file to find the checkout cards for all copies. The checkout cards should be marked in some way. A clip may be used, although clips sometimes fall off or catch other cards. Plastic covers with a colored stripe across the top, which can be purchased from library supply houses, are easy to slip over the checkout card. The library reserve slip will then be placed in its appropriate spot in the circulation file. The slip should be dated so that, if there are several reserves for the same title, the first request will be filled first.

Library Reserve Slip

```
┌─────────────────────────────────────────┐
│                                          │
│      LIBRARY RESERVE SLIP                │
│                                          │
│   Please save this item for me and       │
│   let me know when it comes in:          │
│                                          │
│   Author_____         │
│                                          │
│   Title_____           │
│                                          │
│   _____            │
│                                          │
│   Call No._____          │
│                                          │
│   Student_____          │
│                                          │
│   Room No._____                   │
│   * * * * * * * * * * * * * * * *         │
│   Space below for library use only        │
│                                          │
│   ┌───┬───┬───┬───┬───┬───┐              │
│   Copy nos.│   │   │   │   │   │   │       │
│   ├───┼───┼───┼───┼───┼───┤              │
│   Date due │   │   │   │   │   │   │       │
│   └───┴───┴───┴───┴───┴───┘              │
│                                          │
│   Date notified_____          │
│                                          │
│   Save until_____           │
│                                          │
│                                          │
└─────────────────────────────────────────┘
```

When books are being carded, those with the plastic cover or other mark will be placed on a reserve shelf. At the earliest opportunity, the reserve file should be checked and a pick-up notice sent to the youngster who is next on the waiting list. The original library reserve slip can be placed in the pocket of the item, showing when the book is to be re-shelved or passed along to the next youngster on the waiting list. Usually a few days are allowed for the item to be picked up, since the child may be absent from school.

Pick-Up Notice

COME AND GET IT!

Your library reserve
is waiting for you.

Student_____

Room No._____

We will hold_____

_____(title)

until the close of school on

_____(date)

Book Reserve System Poster

TAKING INVENTORY OF THE SHELVES

School libraries usually do shelf inventory once a year, just after school closes in June or before it opens in September. As the collection grows, it may become too large to be inventoried every year; when this happens, the collection may be divided into two or more sections, and a shelf inventory will be done of one section each year. If a record is kept of the section inventoried each year, each part of the collection can be properly inventoried in its turn.

The shelf inventory is a procedure of checking for missing items by comparing the shelf list with the materials actually on the shelves. The first step is to read the shelves and make sure all items are in correct order.

The easiest way to take inventory is to have two people working together, one reading from the shelf list drawer and the other checking the shelves. The one at the shelves should check each item to be sure that the correct checkout card is in the pocket.

If an item is missing, the shelf list card should be clipped or the item should be noted on a list. The copy number is part of the information necessary on any missing list. Later, the circulation file can be checked, as well as any other likely place where the item might be found. Items which are not located are marked on the shelf list as "missing in inventory" with the date (see shelf list card sample on page 32). If a missing item is located later, the correct copy number must be reinstated on the shelf list card.

Eventually, if the item cannot be found, the librarian will decide whether or not to reorder. Items that are not reordered, and of which no other copies remain in the collection, must be removed both from the shelf list and from the catalog card files.

Sometimes items on the shelf will have no shelf list card, or will have a copy number different from that shown on the shelf list card. These items should be removed from the shelf. They may lack not only shelf list card but catalog cards as well. The library staff will check for both possibilities and take whatever steps are necessary.

REMOVING CATALOG CARDS

When the last copy of any item is lost or discarded and is not to be replaced, the item must be removed both from the shelf list and from the card catalog. Sometimes a central processing office must be notified as well.

The shelf list card can be found in the shelf list file under the call number of the item. Then, in the card catalog, there will be a main entry card filed under the same word that appears first on the shelf list card. That main entry card in turn will indicate at the bottom all the other cards in the catalog file.

If the main entry card is an author card, as is usually the case, there will probably be another card under the title of the book, one or more subject headings (as listed at the bottom of the main entry card), and perhaps cards for one or more joint authors, one or more illustrators, the series of which the book is a part, and so on. All cards should be removed and put with the shelf list card, to be checked by the library staff.

FILING CATALOG CARDS

One of the most demanding tasks in the library is the filing of catalog cards. There is one, and only one, correct place for each card. The rules by which that one place is located are not easy to remember. In fact, the card catalog filer should have the list of rules at hand while he is filing and should look up any rule about which he feels at all uncertain.

Drawers in a card catalog are always arranged in vertical rows beginning at the left side as shown below.

Arrangement of Card Catalog Drawers

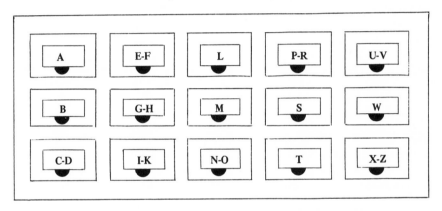

Cards are usually filed above the rod in the drawers and checked by another person, or by the same person at a later time. Once a card has been filed in the wrong place, other cards are likely to be filed incorrectly as well, leading to badly mixed-up drawers and confusion on the part of the students, teachers, and library workers who use the catalog.

A self-teaching unit on filing in the card catalog is presented in Chapter 4. The unit selects from the second edition of the *ALA Rules for Filing Catalog Cards* (Chicago, American Library Association, 1968) those rules that are most likely to be needed in a multi-media school library catalog. Each library should also have a paperback copy of the abridged edition of the ALA filing rules.

An index to the rules in the self-teaching unit is at the back of this book. After completing the unit, consult the index for any rules or examples you may need.

The self-teaching unit is concluded by a comprehensive review problem; you should try to work out this problem once a year, as a means of keeping the important rules in mind.

3 : PUTTING LIBRARY MATERIALS IN ORDER

A Teach-Yourself Unit

BEFORE YOU BEGIN

The format of this unit is sometimes called programmed instruction. It first presents information, then a problem or two so you can check your understanding, and then an immediate opportunity to find out whether you have made any mistakes. It is important to follow all directions carefully and to work out all the problems, no matter how simple they look.

This unit was designed for use in a workshop with volunteers working together in pairs and a librarian available to answer questions. However, it can also be used by one person working alone.

The problem pages will work best if they are photocopied and cut out in advance, with each problem put into an envelope. It is much easier, and more like real shelving, to move the slips of paper around until they are in correct order, than to re-copy all the call numbers with pencil and paper.

Library call numbers vary in different libraries. You may revise this unit and reproduce it in revised form to meet your needs.

SORTING MATERIALS

Most libraries have separate places for each of the following:

Type of Material	Type of Call Number	Example
Fiction books	Letters only, on one line.	ALT
Easy books	The letter E above one or more letters.	E A
Nonfiction books	A number above a letter or letters.	973 L

(continued on next page)

Type of Material	Type of Call Number	Example
Audiovisual materials	Two or three capital letters above the call number. In this example FS means "filmstrip." You may find RD for disc recording, SP for study print, etc.	FS 973 L
Reference materials	R or REF over any of the above call numbers. Reference materials are encyclopedias and other works designed for quick location of specific information.	R 031 W
Professional materials	P over any of the above call numbers. Professional materials are for teachers and other school staff. They are always shelved in a separate location.	P 370 M
Magazines	Usually no call number; filed alphabetically by title and then by date of issue.	
Pamphlets	Usually no call number; filed alphabetically by subject in drawers or boxes; the subject is printed on the front cover of the pamphlet.	

Call number formats sometimes vary. For example, libraries may use any of the following for a fiction book by Smith:

SMI   Smith   F   FIC
                 S   SMI

Look around the library you are working in to see what formats are used.

Notice that we use the term "call number" even when the call number is made up of *letters* only.

If several symbols are combined, the *top one* must be considered first in deciding where to shelve the item.

You will want to look around the library in your school to discover where different types of material are kept.

Go on to page 40.

Problem 1

Here are the call numbers for 24 items ready to be shelved. If possible, photo-copy this page and cut the numbers apart.

POT	398 M	RT POT	FS E H	PAL	973.7 R
CT 612 H	P RT 372.6 L	MCD	E A	SP 551.5 C	P LON
R 031 E	629.2 P	E R	FS 629.2 P	P 371.2 M	R 920 WEB
921 BRO	P R 370 E	ST 910 W	ANN	E F	RD 921 FOS

On page 41 is a "library" divided into six sections. Sort or re-copy the above call numbers into the proper sections of the "library."

Fiction	Easy	Non-Fiction

Reference	Audiovisual	Professional

Now check your answer on page 44.

Go on to page 44.

Have you already checked your answer to Problem 1 on page 44? If not, please turn to page 44 *before* you read this page.

SHELF ARRANGEMENT

Materials are shelved as we read a book:

From the left end of the shelf to the right. . .

ABE	ABR	ACL	ACT	ADE	ADR	AFA	AFF

From the top shelf to the bottom. . .

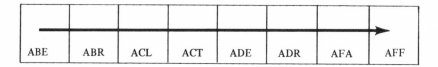

ABE	ABR	ACL	ACT	ADE	ADR	AFA	AFF
AFR	AGA	AGE	AGL	AHO	ALA	ALC	ALD

From the bottom shelf of one section to the top shelf of the next section to the right. . .

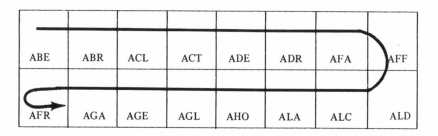

ABE	ABR	ACL	ACT	ADE	ADR	AFA	AFF	AMU	ANN	APR	ARA	ARE	ARL	ARM	ARM
AFR	AGA	AGE	AGL	AHO	ALA	ALC	ALD	ARN	ARR	ART	ASE	ASH	ASH	ASP	ATA
ALD	ALL	AMA	AME	AME	AMO	AMR	AMT	ATU	AVE	AWE	AYE	BAC	BAD	BAG	BAM

Go on to page 43.

SHELVING FICTION BOOKS

Fiction books are kept in alphabetical order by the author's name. The call number on a fiction book is usually the first three letters of the author's last name. Here are some fiction books shelved in proper order.

Ball BAL	Balmer BAL	Baum BAU	Bayle BAY
Mary Carter CAR	Robert Carter CAR	Cather CAT	Caudill CAU

Problem 2

Here are the call numbers for six fiction books. If possible, photocopy this page and cut the call numbers apart. Otherwise, re-copy the call numbers in correct order from left to right.

Mackey MAC	Meyer MEY	Lyons LYO	George McDonald MCD	MacLean MAC	Jean MacDonald MAC

Now check your answer on page 46.

Skip ahead to page 46.

Answer to Problem 1

The call numbers may be in any order. But they must be in the right box. If you have one in the wrong box, please turn back to pages 38 and 39 (Sorting Materials) and see if you can discover why you made a mistake.

Fiction	Easy	Non-fiction
POT	E A	629.2 P
PAL		
	E	921
MCD	R	BRO
ANN	E F	398 M
		973.7 R

Reference	Audiovisual		Professional	
R 031 E	FS 629.2 P	ST 910 W	P 371.2 M	P LON
R 920 WEB	SP 551.5 C	CT 612 H	P RT 372.6 L	
	RT POT	FS E H	P R 370 E	
	RD 921 FOS			

If you had any errors, please turn back to pages 38 and 39 and see if you can discover why you made a mistake. Then go on to page 42.

Turn back to page 42.

SHELVING EASY BOOKS

The E on the top line of the call number comes from the word "Easy." This section often includes picture books as well as easy reading books for children from kindergarten through grade 2 or 3.

The letter on the second line comes from the author's last name. It is not possible to keep these books in exact order by the author's full name most of the time. We just try to keep the A's together, the B's together, and so on.

Some libraries have shelves for the short easy books above shelves for the tall easy books with the same call number.

Here are some easy books shelved in proper order:

E	E	E	E	E	E
A	A	A	B	C	C

Skip ahead to page 47.

Answer to Problem 2

This is the correct arrangement.

Lyons	Jean MacDonald	Mackey	MacLean	George McDonald	Meyer
LYO	MAC	MAC	MAC	MCD	MEY

A special note about Mc names . . . you may perhaps already have learned that in the card catalog names beginning "Mc" and names beginning "Mac" are ALL filed as if they began with *Mac*. You will notice that this has *not* happened on the library shelf above.

Most libraries shelve books as shown here, and file their shelf list cards the same way. At the same time they use the special *Mac* rule in the card catalog.

Sometimes, however, libraries change the call numbers on *Mac* books to match the card catalog rule. In that case the above shelf would come out this way:

Lyons	George McDonald	Jean MacDonald	Mackey	MacLean	Meyer
LYO	MAC	MAC	MAC	MAC	MEY

Notice that the call number has been changed on the book by George McDonald.

When shelving fiction, look at the call number *first*, then at the author's name.

Go back to page 45.

SHELVING NON-FICTION BOOKS

The number part of the call number on a non-fiction book is a Dewey Decimal number. The librarian looks at the subject of a book to decide on its Dewey number.

As much as possible, materials on the same subject come together on the shelves. Materials on related subjects are located close to each other.

A Dewey Decimal number always has at least three digits. These are arranged from the smallest number to the largest.

Here are some Dewey Decimal numbers in correct order from left to right:

599   608   620   621   624

Problem 3

Below are six Dewey Decimal numbers. Photocopy this page and cut the numbers apart, or re-copy them.

Arrange the numbers in correct order from left to right.

133	031	170	220	001	020

Now check your answer on page 50.

Skip ahead to page 50.

Answer to Problem 4

This is the correct arrangement.

624   629   629.2   636.7   640   641.5

LONGER DEWEY NUMBERS

Longer Dewey numbers are also arranged like ordinary decimal numbers. Sometimes this looks confusing.

For example,

> 629.13 comes before 629.2
> because .13 is a smaller decimal number than .2

There is a quick way to check which number comes first when some numbers are longer than others. Just imagine one or more zeros added to the end of the shorter numbers.

Looking back at the example we just had,

> imagine that 629.2 had a zero added.
> Then it would look like 629.20.

It looks all right to have 629.13 before 629.20, so it must be correct to put 629.13 ahead of 629.2.

If that still seems confusing, try this way to look at Dewey numbers. (This way would *not* work in arithmetic. It can work in a library only because a Dewey number always has exactly three digits before the decimal point.)

To use this way, just match the numbers from left to right. As soon as you find a smaller digit, or run out of digits, you have discovered which number comes first.

Go on to page 49.

Look at these numbers. They are *not* in correct order.

913.4   913.35   909   920   891.7   914.2   913

Look at the first digit, the one on the left, in each Dewey number. One of the numbers begins with 8, but all the others begin with 9. So the number beginning with 8 must come first.

891.7 .....

Since all the remaining numbers begin with 9, we must move over to the second digit. One of these numbers has 0 for the second digit, so it must come next.

891.7   909 .....

Four of the remaining numbers have 1 for the second digit. Only one number has a 2. So the number with the 2 must come *last*, at the end of the row.

891.7   909 920

We still have these numbers to fit in between:

913.4   913.35   914.2   913

Again, only one number has 4 for the third digit, so it must come toward the end.

891.7   909 . . . . 914.2   920

Now we go on to the *fourth* digit of the three remaining numbers (913.4, 913.35, and 913) and we find a 4, a 3, and a number where we have run out of digits. Running out of digits is like coming to a zero. So now we can complete the arrangement:

891.7   909   913   913.35   913.4   914.2   920

Skip ahead to page 51.

Answer to Problem 5

891.7   909   913   913.35   913.4   914.2   920

Go on to Problem 6 on page 52.

Answer to Problem 3

This is the correct arrangement.

001   020   031   133   170   220

THE DECIMAL POINT

After the third digit, there is a decimal point before any more digits are added. Dewey Decimal numbers *with* decimal points come between the whole numbers. This is just as ordinary decimal numbers would be placed in arithmetic if we were counting from the smaller number to the larger.

These numbers are in correct order from left to right.

973   973.1   973.3   973.7   974   974.4

Problem 4

Below are six Dewey Decimal numbers, some with decimal points. Photo-copy this page and cut the numbers apart, or re-copy them.

Arrange the numbers in correct order from left to right.

624	629.2	641.5	640	629	636.7

Now check your answer on page 48.

Go back to page 48.

Sorting out Dewey Decimal numbers when some are longer than others is not easy. One must watch carefully.

Here is the same group of numbers we worked with on page 49, but again, not in correct order.

Problem 5

Photocopy this page and cut the numbers apart, or re-copy them. Arrange the numbers in correct order from left to right.

913.4	913.35	909	920
891.7	914.2	913	

Then check your answer by looking back to the *bottom line* on page 49. If you have made a mistake, read page 49 again until you find where you made your error.

Go back to the bottom of page 49.

Problem 6

Here are seven Dewey Decimal numbers, some of them longer than others. Photocopy this page and cut the numbers apart, or re-copy them. Arrange them in correct order from left to right. Then check your answer on page 55.

629.4	629.1	629.2	629
629.13	630	629.22	

Skip ahead to the *bottom* of page 55 and check your answer to Problem 6.

Go on to the bottom of page 55.

Answer to Problem 7

This is the correct arrangement.

914   914.2   917   917.29   917.291   917.3

917.48   917.492   917.495   917.5

COMPLETE NON-FICTION CALL NUMBERS

A letter is added below the Dewey Decimal number to complete a non-fiction call number. The letter usually comes from the author's last name. (Some libraries use two or even three letters below the Dewey Decimal number.)

The letter below the Dewey number is used for shelving *only* if two numbers are exactly alike.

Here are some complete non-fiction call numbers in correct order from left to right.

520   523   523.14   523.8   523.8   525
Z   A   R   L   P   A

The letter was used only to distinguish between the two books numbered 523.8.

Problem 8

Here are five non-fiction call numbers. Photocopy this page and cut the numbers apart, or re-copy them. Arrange them in correct order from left to right.

301.451 A	301.451 C	302.1 L	301.4 L	301.6 R

Now check your answer on page 56.

Skip ahead to page 56.

Answer to Problem 9

This is the correct arrangement.

	Marshall Giants of Science	Martin Composers of Yesterday	Lewis Sam Houston
919.8 S	920 MAR	920 MAR	921 HOU
Smith Elias Howe 921 HOW	Sandburg Abraham Lincoln 921 LIN	Johns Lindbergh 921 LIN	 930 F

SHELVING PROFESSIONAL AND
REFERENCE MATERIALS

Professional materials (P above the call number) are always kept in a separate place. They are for use of teachers and other staff members.

Reference (R or Ref above the call number) and audiovisual materials (FS, RD, or SP above the call number) are often, but not always, kept in a separate section of the library. However, once you get to the right section, these added letters (P, R, FS, etc.) do not change the arrangement of the call numbers. They simply tell you that this item is not an ordinary book.

Go on to Problem 10 on page 55.

Go on to page 55.

Problem 10

Here are five call numbers from the reference section. As before, rearrange these numbers in correct order from left to right. Then check your answer on page 62.

R 032 C	R 423 W	R 031 C vol. 2	R 317.3 I	R 031 C vol. 1

Skip ahead to page 62.

Answer to Problem 6

This is the correct arrangement.

629   629.1   629.13   629.2   629.22   629.4   630

Go on to Problem 7 and try one more of these.

Problem 7

Here are ten Dewey Decimal numbers, some of them longer than others. Photocopy this page and cut the numbers apart or re-copy them. Arrange them in correct order from left to right.

914	917	917.3	917.492	917.5
917.495	914.2	917.291	917.48	917.29

Now check your answer on page 53.

Go back to page 53.

Answer to Problem 8

This is the correct arrangement.

301.4	301.451	301.451	301.6	302.1
L	A	C	R	L

SHELVING BIOGRAPHIES

One part of the non-fiction section needs further explanation—the biography section.

There are two numbers in the biography section:

> 920 is for books that tell the lives of two or more persons. These are *collected* biographies.

> 921 is for books that tell the life of one person or, sometimes, one family. These are *individual* biographies. (Some libraries use 92 or B instead of 921.)

COLLECTED BIOGRAPHIES

Collected biographies often have at least three letters below the number 920. These letters come from the author's last name.

Books numbered 920 are subarranged alphabetically by the author's last name. The following example is in correct order from left to right:

	Allston Famous Flyers	Anderson Ten Heroes	Baldwin American Nurses	Ballard Musicians Today
919 F	920 ALL	920 AND	920 BAL	920 BAL

Go on to page 57.

INDIVIDUAL BIOGRAPHIES

Individual biographies (921, 92 or B) usually have at least three letters below the number. However, these letters come from the *subject's* last name. In this way, all books about the same person come together on the shelves. For example, all books about Joe Namath would have the call number:

921
NAM

Some people do not have a last name in the sense of a family name. For example, a biography of Leonardo da Vinci would have the call number:

921
LEO

A biography of Crazy Horse would have the call number:

921
CRA

Individual biographies are arranged alphabetically by the subject's full name. This keeps together all books or materials about the same person. The following individual biographies are arranged in correct order from left to right:

Turner Franklin Delano Roosevelt 921 ROO	Smith Teddy Roosevelt 921 ROO	Allan Doctor Benjamin Rush 921 RUS	Stewart John Ruskin 921 RUS

Go on to page 58.

Problem 9

Below are shown eight books, including collected and individual biographies. Photocopy this page and cut the rectangles apart, or re-copy them. Arrange them in correct order from left to right.

		Martin Composers of Yesterday 920 MAR	Marshall Giants of Science 920 MAR
919.8 S	930 F		
Sandburg Abraham Lincoln 921 LIN	Johns Lindbergh 921 LIN	Smith Elias Howe 921 HOW	Lewis Sam Houston 921 HOU

Now check your answer on page 54.

Go back to page 54.

Answer to the Review Problem

Fiction Books					
C. S. Lewis	E. Lewis	MacDonald	Madden	McArthur	Meadows
LEW	LEW	MAC	MAD	MCA	MEA

Easy Books			Reference Books		
E K	E L	E M	R 031 W	R 317.3 I	R 920 DIC

Teachers' Professional Shelf			Audiovisual Materials		
P 612.6 B	P FS 612.6 D	P 612.6 H	FS 917 M	FS 917.3 B	FS 918 E

Non-fiction Books					
070 R	292 M	300 R	301.4 A	301.45 L	301.451 I
301.451 W	301.453 D	301.5 B	301.7 L	302 F	920 MOR
		(about Booker T. Washington)	(about George Washington)		
920 SMI	921 WAR	921 WAS	921 WAS	929.9 E	930 H

Now you are ready to shelve materials in your school library. Thank you for helping!

Go on to Chapter 4, page 63.

Review Problem

Here are 36 call numbers to be arranged in the "library" on page 61. Photocopy this page and cut out the squares, or re-copy the call numbers. In the non-fiction section, remember to arrange the shelves as shown on page 42.

E. Lewis LEW	(about George Washington) 921 WAS	FS 917 M	Madden MAD	301.451 I	930 H
Meadows MEA	(about Booker T. Washington) 921 WAS	070 R	R 920 DIC	E M	McArthur MCA
R 031 W	E L	301.45 L	C. S. Lewis LEW	P FS 612.6 D	E K
P 612.6 H	301.451 W	921 WAR	R 317.3 I	301.453 D	P 612.6 B
301.5 B	301.7 L	920 MOR	302 F	FS 918 E	301.4 A
300 R	FS 917.3 B	929.9 E	920 SMI	MacDonald MAC	292 M

This is the "library" for the Review Problem.

Fiction Books				

Easy Books			Reference Books	

Teachers' Professional Shelf			Audiovisual Materials	

Non-fiction Books				

Check your answer on page 59.

Go back to page 59.

Answer to Problem 10

This is the correct arrangement.

R	R	R	R	R
031	031	032	317.3	423
C	C	C	I	W
vol. 1	vol. 2			

When you look in your own school library for the places where professional, reference, and audiovisual materials are kept, be sure to look also for magazine storage and the pamphlet file (sometimes called the vertical file). Check, too, to see where oversize materials too large or flimsy for the regular shelf are stored.

Go back to page 60.

4 : FILING IN THE CARD CATALOG

A Teach-Yourself Unit

BEFORE YOU BEGIN

The format of this unit is sometimes called programmed instruction. It presents information, then a problem or two so you can check your understanding, and then an immediate opportunity to find out whether you have made any mistakes. It is important to follow all directions carefully and to work out all the problems, no matter how simple they look.

This unit was designed for use in a workshop in which volunteers work together in pairs and a librarian is available to answer questions. However, it can be used by one person working alone.

Problems 12 through 16 and the Review Problem are easier to solve if they are photocopied and cut out in advance, with each problem put into an envelope. It is much easier, and more like real filing, to move the slips of paper around until they are in correct order, than to recopy all the headings. (If necessary, type each heading on a separate card and arrange the cards in correct order.)

KINDS OF CATALOG CARDS

There are three basic kinds of catalog cards:

> author,
> title, and
> subject.

Each book usually has:

> one author card,
> one title card, and
> one or more subject cards.

Go on to page 64.

For example, *Misty of Chincoteague* by Marguerite Henry would have:

an author card (Henry, Marguerite) filed in the H's;
a title card (Misty of Chincoteague) filed in the M's; and
a subject card (HORSES–STORIES), also filed in the H's.

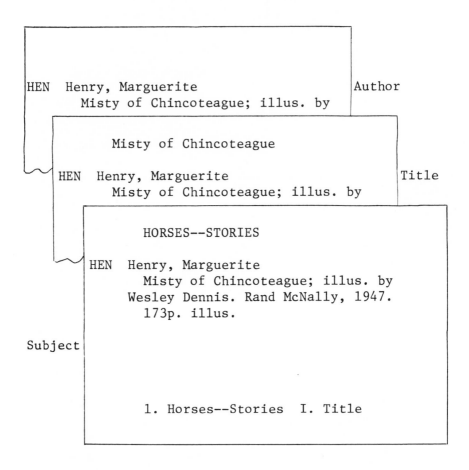

```
HEN   Henry, Marguerite                         Author
         Misty of Chincoteague; illus. by
```

```
         Misty of Chincoteague

    HEN   Henry, Marguerite                      Title
             Misty of Chincoteague; illus. by
```

```
             HORSES--STORIES

        HEN   Henry, Marguerite
                 Misty of Chincoteague; illus. by
              Wesley Dennis. Rand McNally, 1947.
                 173p. illus.




                 1. Horses--Stories  I. Title
```

Subject

Go on to page 65.

Another example, *The Caves of the Great Hunters* by Hans Baumann would have:

> an author card (Baumann, Hans) filed in the B's;
> a title card (The caves of the great hunters) filed in the C's; and
> a subject card (MAN, PREHISTORIC) filed in the M's.

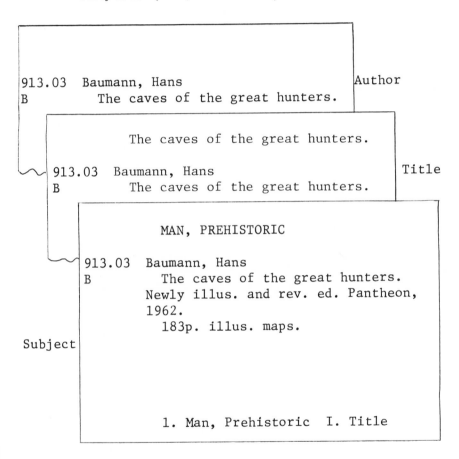

Go on to page 66.

Even though the library may have several copies of a book, there will be only one set of catalog cards.

Sometimes books or audiovisual materials have more cards than those shown above, but the three basic types of cards are author, title, and subject.

KINDS OF HEADINGS

The heading is the top line on a catalog card.

For example, the heading on an author card is the author's name (last name first).

Notice how the headings are printed for the two examples you saw on pages 64 and 65:

Author cards:	Henry, Marguerite
	Baumann, Hans
Title cards:	Misty of Chincoteague
	The caves of the great hunters
Subject cards:	HORSES–STORIES
	MAN, PREHISTORIC

Which type of heading is printed entirely in capital letters? Which is *not* all in capitals, but begins with a person's surname? Did you notice that on the title cards only the first word and proper names (for example, Chincoteague) begin with a capital letter?

Following are four problems. From the way the headings are printed, can you identify which types they are?

Problem 1

What kind of heading are these?   <u>Choose One</u>

Story of ants	author	_____
Treasure Island	title	_____
	subject	_____
	mixed	_____

Check your answer on page 69.

Skip ahead to page 69.

Answer to Problem 3

Both are subject headings.

Problem 4

What kind of heading are these?   <u>Choose One</u>

STORYTELLING   author   _____
ALCOTT, LOUISA MAY   title   _____
                               subject   _____
                               mixed   _____

Check your answer on the *top* of page 68.

Go on to page 68.

Answer to Problem 2

Both are author headings.

Now try Problem 3 on the *bottom* of page 69.

Skip ahead to the bottom of page 69.

Answer to Problem 4

Both are subject headings.

BASIC FILING RULES

In a dictionary catalog, all kinds of cards are interfiled. The six headings shown on page 66 would be filed this way:

> Baumann, Hans
> The caves of the great hunters
> Henry, Marguerite
> HORSES–STORIES
> MAN, PREHISTORIC
> Misty of Chincoteague

The card at the top of the list would be nearest the front of the drawer.

> †† The basic arrangement is alphabetical, word by word.

"Word by word" filing means that a space must be considered. A space counts as "nothing" or "zero," and "nothing" comes before the letter A just as zero comes before the number 1.

This way:	**Not** this way:
In the days of giants	INCAS
INCAS	In the days of giants
This way:	**Not** this way:
Dog of Flanders	Doggone roan
Doggone roan	Dog of Flanders

Problem 5

Which arrangement is correct—A or B?

A	**B**
I met a man	If wishes were horses
If wishes were horses	I met a man

Check your answer on page 70.

Go on to page 70.

Answer to Problem 1

Both are title headings.

Problem 2

What kind of heading are these?   <u>Choose One</u>

    Alcott, Louisa May   author   —————

    Fisher, Aileen   title   —————

                              subject —————

                              mixed   —————

Check your answer on the *bottom* of page 67.

Go back to the bottom of page 67.

Problem 3

What kind of heading are these?   <u>Choose One</u>

    SNAKES   author   —————

    U.S.–HISTORY   title   —————

                              subject —————

                              mixed   —————

Check your answer on the *top* of page 67.

Go back to the top of page 67.

Answer to Problem 5

Arrangement A is correct.

---

†† Ignore capitalization and most punctuation marks.

Problem 6

Which arrangement is correct—A or B?

A	**B**
MEAT	Me, myself and I
Me, myself and I	MEAT

Check your answer on the *bottom* of page 71.

Go on to the bottom of page 71.

Answer to Problem 7

Arrangement B is correct.

Go on to the bottom of page 72.

Answer to Problem 8

Arrangement B is correct.

Problem 9

Which arrangement is correct—A or B?

A	**B**
Latin America today	LATIN AMERICAN POETRY
LATIN AMERICAN POETRY	Latin America today

Check your answer on page 73.

Go on to page 73.

Answer to Problem 6

Arrangement B is correct.

Go on to page 72.

Problem 7

Which arrangement is correct—A or B?

A	**B**
Smithers, John	Smith, John
Smith, John	Smithers, John

Check your answer on the *bottom* of page 70.

Go back to the bottom of page 70.

---

†† A dash separates words. It is filed like a space.

This way: **Not** this way:
   HORSES–STORIES   Horses think smart
   Horses think smart   HORSES–STORIES

Reminder: In all examples, the heading at the *top* of each list would come nearest the *front* of the drawer in the card catalog.

Problem 8

Which arrangement is correct—A or B?

A	**B**
Rome of today	ROME–HISTORY
ROME–HISTORY	Rome of today

Check your answer on the *top* of page 71.

Go back to the top of page 71.

Answer to Problem 9

Arrangement A is correct.

Problem 10

Which arrangement is correct—A, B, C, or D?

A
EDUCATION
EDUCATION–AIMS AND
    OBJECTIVES
Educational theories
EDUCATION, ANCIENT
Education and American
    civilization
Educationese
EDUCATION, MEDIEVAL
Education through art
EDUCATION–U.S.

B
EDUCATION
EDUCATION–AIMS AND
    OBJECTIVES
EDUCATION, ANCIENT
EDUCATION, MEDIEVAL
EDUCATION–U.S.
Education and American
    civilization
Education through art
Educational theories
Educationese

C
EDUCATION
EDUCATION–AIMS AND
    OBJECTIVES
EDUCATION, ANCIENT
Education and American
    civilization
EDUCATION, MEDIEVAL
Education through art
EDUCATION–U.S.
Educational theories
Educationese

D
EDUCATION
EDUCATION–AIMS AND
    OBJECTIVES
EDUCATION–U.S.
EDUCATION, ANCIENT
EDUCATION, MEDIEVAL
Education and American
    civilization
Education through art
Educational theories
Educationese

Check your answer on page 74.

Go on to page 74.

Answer to Problem 10

Group C is correct.

Problem 11

Which arrangement is correct—A, B, C, or D?

A

New York (Archdiocese)
NEW YORK (BATTLESHIP)
New York (City)
NEW YORK (CITY)–
CHARITIES
NEW YORK (CITY)–
DESCRIPTION
NEW YORK (COUNTY)
New York Academy of Medicine
New York and the Seabury
investigation
New York Business Development
Corporation
New York City Council of
Political Reform

B

New York Academy of Medicine
New York and the Seabury
investigation
New York (Archdiocese)
NEW YORK (BATTLESHIP)
New York Business Development
Corporation
New York (City)
NEW YORK (CITY)–
CHARITIES
New York City Council of
Political Reform
NEW YORK (CITY)–
DESCRIPTION
NEW YORK (COUNTY)

C

NEW YORK (BATTLESHIP)
NEW YORK (CITY)–
CHARITIES
NEW YORK (CITY)–
DESCRIPTION
NEW YORK (COUNTY)
New York Academy of Medicine
New York and the Seabury
investigation
New York (Archdiocese)
New York Business Development
Corporation
New York (City)
New York City Council of
Political Reform

D

NEW YORK (BATTLESHIP)
NEW YORK (CITY)–
CHARITIES
NEW YORK (CITY)–
DESCRIPTION
NEW YORK (COUNTY)
New York (Archdiocese)
New York (City)
New York Academy of Medicine
New York and the Seabury
investigation
New York Business Development
Corporation
New York City Council of
Political Reform

Check your answer on page 76.

Go on to page 76.

†† File **abbreviations** as if the word were spelled out in full.

File Dr. like Doctor.
File Mr. like Mister.
BUT Mrs. is filed just as it is spelled!

†† **Numbers and symbols** are filed as if they were spelled out in words.

File Art & commonsense like Art and commonsense.
File 5:30 like Five-thirty.
File '49-ers like Forty-niners.
File 1984 like Nineteen eighty-four.
File 112 dinosaurs like One hundred and twelve dinosaurs.
File 112 Elm St. like One-twelve Elm Street.
File $20.00 like Twenty dollars.
File 20,000 like Twenty thousand.

What about hyphens?

†† **A hyphen** joins words together.

If either of the two parts cannot stand alone as a separate word and keep its meaning, ignore the hyphen and file as one word.

But if both parts can stand alone with the same meaning, file the hyphen like a space.

File Co-operation like Cooperation.
File Epoch-making like Epoch making.
File Saint-Gaudens (a person's last name) like Saint Gaudens.

Go on to page 77.

Answer to Problem 11

Group B is correct. All entries are filed in straight alphabetical order, word by word, disregarding most punctuation including dashes and parentheses.

You have now learned the basic filing rules.

SPECIAL RULES

There are, however, some questions and exceptions that come up often in a school library.

Read through the following rules and examples until you come to Problem 12. Then look back at these pages as often as you need to while you work out that problem.

What about abbreviations, initials, and other symbols?

> †† Arrange **most initials** as if each initial were a one-letter word.

File AAA like A A A.
File AAAS Conference like A A A S Conference.
File A. B. C. programs like A B C programs.

> †† But **geographic initials** are filed as if the geographic name were spelled out in full.

File USSR like Union of Soviet Socialist Republics.
File U.S. like United States.

> †† File **acronyms** like one word. Acronyms are sets of initials which are pronounced like a word.

File FORTRAN like Fortran.
File UNESCO like Unesco.
File UNICEF like Unicef.

Go back to page 75.

Problem 12

Pages 77 through 81 show 36 headings from catalog cards. Photocopy these pages, cut apart the headings and rearrange them. As you work, look back at pages 75 and 76 as often as you need to.

When you think you have the problem in correct order, check your work on page 82. The heading at the *top* of your list should be the one that would come nearest to the *front* of the card catalog file.

... And beat him when he sneezes

Boy's book of body building

U.S.–GOVERNMENT AND POLITICS

St. Clair, Robert

Doctoring among the Indians

Whodunit?

Go on to page 78.

Problem 12 (Cont'd)

Who is who in music?
U. D. F.
Mis-working equipment
1,000 questions
Who's who?
Mrs. Miniver
Co-operation in government
Boys & girls at school

Go on to page 79.

Problem 12 (Cont'd)

MONKEYS
Mr. Adam
Hall of fame
And now good-bye
Boy trouble
1035 Elm Street
SOUTH CAROLINA
Dr. Jekyll and Mr. Hyde

Go on to page 80.

Problem 12 (Cont'd)

Boys' and girls' games
CONCORD, VT.
Ten little Indians
Ubangis
Unemployment
UNESCO
Boys will be boys
CONCORD, VA.

Go on to page 81.

Problem 12 (Cont'd)

Hall-Edwards, John
10:35 train
101 games
United States and Russia
St. Mary's Church
United States in the modern world

Check your answer on page 82.

Go on to page 82.

Answer to Problem 12

The first "card" at the top of this list would be the one nearest the front in the card catalog drawer.

... And beat him when he sneezes
And now good-bye
Boy trouble
Boys & girls at school
Boys' and girls' games
Boy's book of body building
Boys will be boys
CONCORD, VT.
CONCORD, VA.
Co-operation in government
Dr. Jekyll and Mr. Hyde
Doctoring among the Indians
Hall-Edwards, John
Hall of fame
Mr. Adam
Mis-working equipment
MONKEYS
Mrs. Miniver
101 games
1,000 questions
St. Clair, Robert
St. Mary's Church
SOUTH CAROLINA
Ten little Indians
1035 Elm Street
10:35 train
U. D. F.
Ubangis
Unemployment
UNESCO
United States and Russia
U.S.–GOVERNMENT AND POLITICS
United States in the modern world
Who is who in music
Whodunit?
Who's who?

Go on to page 83.

Continue reading until you come to Problem 13. Then look back at these pages as often as you need to while you work out that problem.

What if there is more than one book by one author?

†† When there is more than one book listed by the same author, file first by author, **then** by title.

Example:

ALBATROSSES
Alcott, Louisa May//Eight cousins
Alcott, Louisa May//Little men
Alcott, Louisa May//Little women
And then there were none

(We are using the double slash // to indicate the part of the information that comes on the next line down on the catalog card.)

What if there is more than one book on exactly the same subject?

†† When more than one card has exactly the same subject heading, arrange first by subject, then by main entry (usually the author). If there are two books under one subject also by the same author, subarrange by title.

Example:

BIRDS//Animals—helpful and harmful
BIRDS//Blough, Glenn O.//Bird watchers
BIRDS//Peterson, Roger Tory//Field guide to the birds
BIRDS//Peterson, Roger Tory//Field guide to the Western birds
BIRDS//Selsam, Millicent E.//Egg to chick

Go on to page 84.

How are cards for audiovisual materials filed?

> †† Cards for **audiovisual materials** are filed like any other cards—up to the parentheses that enclose the type of medium.

The only problem arises when book and audiovisual cards have the same headings

> †† If exactly the same heading appears for book and non-book materials, put the book first.

Example:

Poe, Edgar Allan//The tell-tale heart
Poe, Edgar Allan//The tell-tale heart (Disc recording)

> †† If the same heading appears in more than one audiovisual medium, arrange alphabetically by the medium.

Example:

Poe, Edgar Allan//The tell-tale heart (Disc recording)
Poe, Edgar Allan//The tell-tale heart (Tape recording)

> †† Otherwise, alphabetize **only** up to the first parenthesis, and ignore all information beyond that point.

Example:

Poe, Edgar Allan//The tell-tale heart
Poe, Edgar Allan//The tell-tale heart (Disc recording)
Poe, Edgar Allan//The tell-tale heart (Tape recording)
Poe, Edgar Allan//The tell-tale heart and other stories

Go on to page 85.

Problem 13

On this page and pages 86 and 87 are 16 headings from catalog cards. Photocopy these pages and cut apart the headings. Then rearrange them. As you work, look back at pages 83 and 84 as often as you need to.

Birds of America
Grassroot jungles
INSECTICIDES
Birds of America (Filmstrips)
BIRD SONG
INSECTS Hylander, Clarence J. Insects on parade
BIRDS–U.S.

Go on to page 86.

Problem 13 (Cont'd)

Insects on parade
Teale, Edwin Way   Grassroot jungles
Whitman, Walt   Leaves of grass (Disc recording)
Junior book of insects
Teale, Edwin Way   Junior book of insects
Whitman, Walt   Leaves of grass
INSECTS Teale, Edwin Way   Grassroot jungles
Whitman, Walt   Leaves of grass (Tape recording)

Go on to page 87.

Problem 13 (Cont'd)

INSECTS

Teale, Edwin Way
Junior book of insects

Now check your answer on page 89.

Skip ahead to page 89.

Skip ahead to page 89.

> †† The same rule applies to articles in titles
> in a **foreign language**.

This way:
EMBROIDERY
El español comercial

Not this way:
El español comercial
EMBROIDERY

> †† Disregard an article also if it is the first word in a **subject heading**.
>
> Also disregard an article if it follows a dash in a subject heading.

This way:
Trouble in the city
THE WEST–HISTORY

Not this way:
THE WEST–HISTORY
Trouble in the city

This way:
AGRICULTURE–U.S.
AGRICULTURE–THE WEST

Not this way:
AGRICULTURE–THE WEST
AGRICULTURE–U.S.

> †† **Do** regard an article at the beginning of a **foreign proper name**.
>
> Other than this case, foreign articles are filed like articles in English.

File De la Roche, John like Delaroche, John.
File Aulaire, Ingri d' like Aulaire, Ingri d'.

Skip ahead to page 90.

Answer to Problem 13

BIRD SONG
Birds of America
Birds of America (Filmstrips)
BIRDS—U.S.
Grassroot jungles
INSECTICIDES
INSECTS//Hylander, Clarence J.//Insects on parade
INSECTS//Teale, Edwin Way//Grassroot jungles
INSECTS//Teale, Edwin Way//Junior book of insects
Insects on parade
Junior book of insects
Teale, Edwin Way//Grassroot jungles
Teale, Edwin Way//Junior book of insects
Whitman, Walt//Leaves of grass
Whitman, Walt//Leaves of grass (Disc recording)
Whitman, Walt//Leaves of grass (Tape recording)

EXCEPTIONS

Problems 12 and 13 have dealt with special questions in applying the basic rules. There are, however, certain exceptions to the basic rules which come up quite often in a school library.

Several of these exceptions deal with *articles*. Articles in English are the three words: a, an, the. Articles in foreign languages are the equivalents to those three words.

> †† Disregard an **article** (a, an, or the) if it is the **first word in a title**. But **do** pay attention to an article in the middle of a title.

This way:
  Man and boy
  A man of his time

Not this way:
  A man of his time
  Man and boy

This way:
  Man of mark
  Man of the ages

Not this way:
  Man of the ages
  Man of mark

Go back to page 88.

Problem 14

On this page and page 91 are 13 headings from catalog cards. Photocopy these pages and cut apart the headings. Then rearrange them. As you work, look back at pages 88 and 89 as often as you need to.

APACHE INDIANS
LA SALLE, ROBERT CAVALIER, SIEUR DE
THE WEST—HISTORY
NATURAL HISTORY—VERMONT
NATURAL HISTORY—THE WEST
De la Mare, Walter

Go on to page 91.

Go on to page 91.

Problem 14 (Cont'd)

Work for Julie
La plume de ma tante
Mann, Thomas
An April after
Man of victory
Work for the beginner
Man of the world

Now check your answer on page 93.

Skip ahead to page 93.

†† Disregard **designations** like "ed." (editor) and "illus." (illustrator) after a name. Subarrange all items done by one person according to title, even if another author name is given.

Example:

> Raskin, Ellen//And it rained
> Raskin, Ellen, illus.//Razzell, A. G.//Circles and curves
> Raskin, Ellen//Ghost in a four-room apartment
> Raskin, Ellen, illus.//Morrow, Suzanne Stark//Inatuk's friends

(To avoid confusion later on, it is a good idea to cross through lightly with pencil the name which is to be disregarded. In the above example, then, one would cross through Razzell's name on the second item and through Morrow's name on the last item. This would show that the cards are subarranged by title.)

†† Arrange the prefixes **M'**, **Mc**, and **Mac** as if they were spelled Mac.

File M'Cormick like Maccormick.
File McCormick like Maccormick.
File MacCormick like Maccormick.

Notice that they all come out alike in this case. Many libraries do not use this rule in placing materials on the shelves or in filing shelf list cards. But the rule is *always* used in the card catalog.

†† Disregard **Roman numerals** after a given name. However, if two such names are otherwise the same, sub-arrange them in numerical order.

Example:

> Charles II, King of France
> Charles I, King of Great Britain
> Charles II, King of Great Britain

Skip ahead to page 94.

Answer to Problem 14

APACHE INDIANS
An April after
De la Mare, Walter
LA SALLE, ROBERT CAVALIER, SIEUR DE
Man of the world
Man of victory
Mann, Thomas
NATURAL HISTORY—VERMONT
NATURAL HISTORY—THE WEST
La plume de ma tante
THE WEST—HISTORY
Work for Julie
Work for the beginner

Several exceptions to the basic rules have to do with *personal names.*

---

†† A one-word personal surname comes **before** all other
headings beginning with the same word.

This way:
    Smith, William
    Smith of Wootton Major
    Smithers, Allan

Not this way:
    Smith of Wootton Major
    Smith, William
    Smithers, Allan

This way:
    Hall, Michael
    Hall Edwards, John

Not this way:
    Hall Edwards, John
    Hall, Michael

---

†† Arrange items **by** an author before items **about** an
author. Or to put it another way, put author cards for
an author before subject cards for the same author.

This way:
    Alcott, Louisa May
    ALCOTT, LOUISA MAY

Go back to page 92.

Problem 15

On this page and pages 95 and 96 are 21 headings from catalog cards. Photo-copy these pages and cut apart the headings. Then rearrange them. As you work, look at pages 92 and 93 as often as you need to.

VICTOR EMMANUEL IV, KING OF ATLANTIS
M'Donald, Peter
MACHINERY
WHITMAN, WALT
WEST, WILLIAM
Saint, Lawrence B.
West, William, illus. Wise, Mary 　　Memories

Go on to page 95.

Problem 15 (Cont'd)

VICTOR EMMANUEL III, KING OF ITALY
Saint-Exupéry, Antoine de
McKenzie, Garry
MacDonald, Robert
Whitman, Walter J.
West African botany
West, William, ed.   Russia
McDONALD, PETER J.

Go on to page 96.

Problem 15 (Cont'd)

Saints and sinners
THE WEST
West, William Today
Machetanz, Frederick
VICTOR EMMANUEL II, KING OF ITALY
Whitman, Walt Complete poetry

Now check your answer on page 97.

Go on to page 97.

Answer to Problem 15

M'Donald, Peter
McDONALD, PETER J.
MacDonald, Robert
Machetanz, Frederick
MACHINERY
McKenzie, Garry
Saint, Lawrence B.
Saint-Exupéry, Antoine de
Saints and sinners
VICTOR EMMANUEL IV, KING OF ATLANTIS
VICTOR EMMANUEL II, KING OF ITALY
VICTOR EMMANUEL III, KING OF ITALY
West, William, illus.//Wise, Mary//Memories
West, William, ed.//Russia
West, William//Today
WEST, WILLIAM
THE WEST
West African botany
Whitman, Walt//Complete poetry
WHITMAN, WALT
Whitman, Walter J.

Go on to page 98.

Go on to page 98.

Another special rule has to do with subjects that have chronological (time period) subdivisions.

> †† When subject cards beginning with the same word or words are subdivided by **time period**:
>
> First, file the subject without subdivisions.
> Then, file the subject subdivided chronologically (by time periods).
> Third, file the subject subdivided by other words.

When filing chronologically, the earliest time period comes first. Sometimes the dates are not given on the card, and in that case, one must find out what those dates are. Fortunately, this usually does not happen except for the United States.

Sometimes two cards begin with the same year, but end with different years. In that case, put the longest time period ahead of the shorter one.

The example below is from U.S. history because this is the one most likely to come up in a school library.

Example:

        U.S.–HISTORY
        U.S.–HISTORY–COLONIAL PERIOD
        U.S.–HISTORY–KING WILLIAM'S WAR, 1689-1697
        U.S.–HISTORY–FRENCH AND INDIAN WAR, 1755-1763
        U.S.–HISTORY–REVOLUTION
        U.S.–HISTORY–REVOLUTION–CAMPAIGNS AND BATTLES
        U.S.–HISTORY–REVOLUTION–SOURCES
        U.S.–HISTORY–1783-1865
        U.S.–HISTORY–CONFEDERATION, 1783-1789
        U.S.–HISTORY–1801-1809
        U.S.–HISTORY–WAR OF 1812
        U.S.–HISTORY–CIVIL WAR
        U.S.–HISTORY–1865-
        U.S.–HISTORY–1865-1898
        U.S.–HISTORY–1898-
        U.S.–HISTORY–WAR OF 1898
        U.S.–HISTORY–20TH CENTURY
        U.S.–HISTORY–1933-1945
        U.S.–HISTORY–BIBLIOGRAPHY
        U.S. history bonus book
        U.S.–HISTORY, MILITARY

Go on to page 99.

Problem 16

Here are nine headings from catalog cards. Photocopy this page and cut apart the headings. Then rearrange them. As you work, look at page 98 as often as you need to.

United States foreign policy
U.S.–FOREIGN RELATIONS–1783-1865
U.S.–FOREIGN RELATIONS–20TH CENTURY
U.S.–FOREIGN RELATIONS–ARABIA
U.S.–FOREIGN RELATIONS–1961-1963–ADDRESSES, ESSAYS, LECTURES
U.S.–FOREIGN RELATIONS–1961-1963
U.S.–FOREIGN RELATIONS–REVOLUTION
U.S.–FOREIGN RELATIONS–ADDRESSES, ESSAYS, LECTURES
U.S.–FOREIGN RELATIONS–CONSTITUTIONAL PERIOD, 1789-1809

Now check your answer on page 100.

Go on to page 100.

Answer to Problem 16

United States foreign policy
U.S.–FOREIGN RELATIONS–REVOLUTION
U.S.–FOREIGN RELATIONS–1783-1865
U.S.–FOREIGN RELATIONS–CONSTITUTIONAL PERIOD, 1789-1809
U.S.–FOREIGN RELATIONS–20TH CENTURY
U.S.–FOREIGN RELATIONS–1961-1963
U.S.–FOREIGN RELATIONS–1961-1963–ADDRESSES, ESSAYS,
    LECTURES
U.S.–FOREIGN RELATIONS–ADDRESSES, ESSAYS, LECTURES
U.S.–FOREIGN RELATIONS–ARABIA

Go on to page 101.

Go on to page 101.

The filing rules you have learned are taken from the second edition of the *ALA Rules for Filing Catalog Cards*, published in 1968. Only those rules most likely to be needed in a school library have been presented.

Remember that there is one, and only one, correct place for any card. If the rules in this self-teaching unit do not show which of two cards should come first, you may want to refer to the complete set of rules. There is a shorter (abridged) paperback edition and a longer (complete) hardbound edition; both are available from the American Library Association, 50 East Huron Street, Chicago, Illinois.

When you are filing, you will not always remember all the rules. But you will probably remember that there is some sort of rule about this or that, and you will want to look it up. To help you do that, an index to this self-teaching unit is provided at the back of this book.

A review problem is given on the following pages of this handbook, so that you can check yourself out on the rules from time to time. It would be a good idea to do the review problem once a year just to remind yourself of the rules. If you can do the review problem correctly, you know all the rules in this self-teaching unit.

Filing catalog cards is a difficult task that requires concentration and patience. Thank you for being willing to do it!

Go on to page 102.

A COMPREHENSIVE REVIEW

This review is a self-check for all the filing rules presented in Chapter 4. After you have completed the 16 problems on filing catalog cards, take a break, then test yourself with this review. If necessary, refer to the filing rules in the teach-yourself unit (pp. 63-101). An index to the rules is at the back of this book. A card catalog filer is not expected to remember all the rules—just that there *is* a rule for a particular case. It is helpful to do this review problem once a year to refresh your memory on important filing rules.

The review contains 92 "catalog cards." Photocopy these pages, cut the cards apart, and arrange them in correct order. Check your answer on pages 114-116.

Review Problem

De la Mare, Walter
2 by 2, to the zoo
TREES–POETRY
HISTORY–PHILOSOPHY
GERMANY–HISTORY–1789-1900
Hey! what's wrong with this one?

Go on to page 103.

Review Problem (Cont'd)

Hall-Smith, Samuel

MINES AND MINERAL RESOURCES—THE WEST

Hall, John
    Science for today

U.S.—DESCRIPTION AND TRAVEL

HISTORY, ANCIENT

Beard, William
From the beginning

Mis-information abounds

HENRY FREDERICK, PRINCE OF WALES

Hall, John, illus.

Adams, Susan
Numbers are fun

Go on to page 104.

Review Problem (Cont'd)

United in one body
SEALS (ANIMALS)
Kipling, Rudyard   Kim
GERMANY–HISTORY–20TH CENTURY
The Federal Bureau of Investigation
HISTORY, ANCIENT Beard, Charles   World before writing
Seals in California
Mr. Popper's penguins

Go on to page 105.

Review Problem (Cont'd)

HALL, JOHN
Debits and credits
Trees and trails
Over the hill
Kipling, Rudyard   The jungle book illustrated
Facts and figures
HISTORY, ANCIENT Beard, Charles   Ancient history
Newspapers in our colonies

Go on to page 106.

Review Problem (Cont'd)

McDonald, Alice

Hall, John, illus.

Martin, Alice
The globe we live on

United States catalog

MINES AND MINERAL RESOURCES—U.S.

Henry, Joseph

HENRY, PATRICK

GERMANY—DESCRIPTION AND TRAVEL—POETRY

An historical atlas of the world

Go on to page 107.

Review Problem (Cont'd)

History of Rome
GERMANY–HISTORY–20TH CENTURY–FICTION
Hall, John, comp.   The best from Science Today
Hey and ho
10:00 train
La mancha
HENRY III, EMPEROR OF THE HOLY ROMAN EMPIRE
UNICEF and you

Go on to page 108.

Review Problem (Cont'd)

GERMANY—HISTORY—PICTORIAL WORKS

OVERLAND JOURNEYS TO THE PACIFIC

Kipling, Rudyard
    The jungle book caravan

Misty of Chincoteague

HENRY VIII, KING OF ENGLAND

Hall behind the curtain

And tomorrow is new

Trees stand tall

Go on to page 109.

Review Problem (Cont'd)

MacDonald, Betty
Money to burn

GERMANY–HISTORY–1918-1933

GERMANY–HISTORY

HISTORY, ANCIENT

Beard, Charles
The rise of Rome

NEW ZEALAND

Kipling, Rudyard
The jungle book (Tape recording)

Henry and Beezus

HENRY II, KING OF ENGLAND

Go on to page 110.

Review Problem (Cont'd)

THE WEST
GERMANY–HISTORY, NAVAL
MacDonald, Betty   Mrs. Piggle-Wiggle
GERMANY–HISTORY–DICTIONARIES
Facts because they're fun
Henry! jump high!
Historical atlas of travel
SEALS (NUMISMATICS)

Go on to page 111.

Review Problem (Cont'd)

HENRY IV, KING OF GERMANY
Hall Edwards, Susan
Twyla
Seals, John
HISTORY, MODERN
Mrs. Malaprop
FBI story
HISTORY, ANCIENT The world of Rome (Filmstrips)

Go on to page 112.

Review Problem (Cont'd)

Misdemeanors and felonies
HENRY, SIR EDWARD RICHARD, BART.
2001
Hall, John, ed.   Adventures with science
Two-tone autos
2 by 2, to William's crew
M'Donald, Barbara
Mister Zap

Go on to page 113.

Review Problem (Cont'd)

GERMANY—FICTION
HISTORY—DICTIONARIES
A new kind of time
Kipling, Rudyard   The jungle book (Filmstrips)
Hallmark cards
GERMANY—HISTORY—1871-1918

Now check your answer on pages 114, 115, and 116. The card at the top of the list would be nearest the front of the card catalog file.

This pack of 92 "catalog cards" to file includes some that are more difficult than the ones you would find in several months of actual filing in a school library, so do not be discouraged if you have one or two wrong. But do check back with the rules to find out why you made your mistake.

Go on to page 114.

Answer to Review Problem

And tomorrow is new
Debits and credits
De la Mare, Walter
FBI story
Facts and figures
Facts because they're fun
The Federal Bureau of Investigation
GERMANY–DESCRIPTION AND TRAVEL–POETRY
GERMANY–FICTION
GERMANY–HISTORY
GERMANY–HISTORY–1789-1900
GERMANY–HISTORY–1871-1918
GERMANY–HISTORY–20TH CENTURY
GERMANY–HISTORY–20TH CENTURY–FICTION
GERMANY–HISTORY–1918-1933
GERMANY–HISTORY–DICTIONARIES
GERMANY–HISTORY, NAVAL
GERMANY–HISTORY–PICTORIAL WORKS
Hall, John, ed.//Adventures with science
Hall, John, comp.//The best from Science Today
Hall, John, illus.//Martin, Alice//The globe we live on
Hall, John, illus.//Adams, Susan//Numbers are fun
Hall, John//Science for today
HALL, JOHN
Hall behind the curtain
Hall Edwards, Susan
Hall-Smith, Samuel
Hallmark cards
HENRY, SIR EDWARD RICHARD, BART.
Henry, Joseph
HENRY, PATRICK
Henry and Beezus
HENRY III, EMPEROR OF THE HOLY ROMAN EMPIRE
HENRY FREDERICK, PRINCE OF WALES
Henry! jump high!
HENRY II, KING OF ENGLAND
HENRY VIII, KING OF ENGLAND
HENRY IV, KING OF GERMANY
Hey and ho
Hey! what's wrong with this one?
An historical atlas of the world
Historical atlas of travel
HISTORY, ANCIENT//Beard, Charles//Ancient history

Go on to page 115.

Answer to Review Problem (Cont'd)

HISTORY, ANCIENT//Beard, Charles//The rise of Rome
HISTORY, ANCIENT//Beard, Charles//World before writing
HISTORY, ANCIENT//Beard, William//From the beginning
HISTORY, ANCIENT//The world of Rome (Filmstrips)
HISTORY–DICTIONARIES
HISTORY, MODERN
History of Rome
HISTORY–PHILOSOPHY
Kipling, Rudyard//The jungle book (Filmstrips)
Kipling, Rudyard//The jungle book (Tape recording)
Kipling, Rudyard//The jungle book caravan
Kipling, Rudyard//The jungle book illustrated
Kipling, Rudyard//Kim
McDonald, Alice
M'Donald, Barbara
MacDonald, Betty//Money to burn
MacDonald, Betty//Mrs. Piggle-Wiggle
La mancha
MINES AND MINERAL RESOURCES–U.S.
MINES AND MINERAL RESOURCES–THE WEST
Misdemeanors and felonies
Mis-information abounds
Mr. Popper's penguins
Mister Zap
Misty of Chincoteague
Mrs. Malaprop
A new kind of time
NEW ZEALAND
Newspapers in our colonies
Over the hill
OVERLAND JOURNEYS TO THE PACIFIC
Seals, John
SEALS (ANIMALS)
Seals in California
SEALS (NUMISMATICS)
10:00 train
Trees and trails
TREES–POETRY
Trees stand tall
2 by 2, to the zoo
2 by 2, to William's crew
2001
Two-tone autos

Go on to page 116.

Answer to Review Problem (Cont'd)

Twyla
UNICEF and you
United in one body
United States catalog
U.S.–DESCRIPTION AND TRAVEL
THE WEST

Go on to page 117.

IN CONCLUSION

We have considered some of the arguments for a multi-media library, which can bring a wide range of high quality books, magazines, recordings, art reproductions, films and filmstrips, and other materials to elementary school children. We have shared with you a bit of the dynamic interplay of materials and users; teachers, library workers, and children; routine procedures and creative program ideas in the school library setting. Many ingredients are orchestrated into a program designed to provide information, offer aesthetic experience, and help children develop social skills and responsibilities.

Your contribution of time and thought to this component of the school can make it significantly more effective. Rarely can a school manage to staff its library in accordance with recent American Library Association standards. Often, in fact, a school librarian must try to manage library operations and programs in two or more buildings with little or no paid clerical help. You can release the librarian to provide a more exciting, more personal, program for the children of your community by giving your time to perform the numerous detailed routines that must be carried out repeatedly. Like housework, library work is never done! Moreover, through sharing your own hobbies and talents, you can enrich the library program in creative ways.

Perhaps you have a flair for art and would like to take displays and bulletin boards as your particular responsibility. Or for music, and could share musical story hours. Perhaps you like the meticulous attention to detail that is required for filing catalog cards, and you will volunteer for that task. (If you do, keep this book handy and make use of the index to the filing rules. And do the review problem from time to time, to keep yourself in trim.) Your typing skills may make you a welcome volunteer in the processing area at your school or in a district processing center. Or perhaps your knack for organization makes you a natural candidate for library chairman.

As you become more involved with the library program, you may want to learn more. A brief list of sources and resources is provided at the back of this book to get you started. Your county or state department of education can probably lend you materials to read. Some community or junior colleges offer courses in library technology. University extension courses—including correspondence courses—deal with children's literature and aspects of library operation. If you are a college graduate, your fascination may lead you to a university department in library science. Occasionally volunteering becomes the first step toward a new career.

In the last few years there has been a strong movement toward community involvement in schools. At one time in our history the school was a social center, where spelling bees and recitations were an important community event. Today, however, community members want to have a say in the goals of their schools, and they are willing to give their time to help the school meet those goals. Mothers and grandmothers, college students and retirees, professionals and laborers—all offer voluntary help to their neighborhood schools. Many volunteers find the school library to be the most rewarding place to become involved. And the beneficiaries are the children of your community.

SOURCES AND RESOURCES

ASSOCIATIONS AND ORGANIZATIONS

American Library Association, 50 East Huron Street, Chicago, Illinois 60611.

The ALA publishes a number of books and pamphlets. Three of these and one of their journals are listed below. You will probably want to request their catalog of books and pamphlets.

ALA Rules for Filing Catalog Cards. 2nd ed. Chicago, American Library Association, 1969.

ALA Rules for Filing Catalog Cards. 2nd ed., abridged. Chicago, American Library Association, 1968.

Hodges, Elizabeth D., comp. *Books for Elementary School Libraries: An Initial Collection.* Chicago, American Library Association, 1969.

National Congress of Parents and Teachers and Children's Services Division, American Library Association. *Let's Read Together: Books for Family Enjoyment.* 3rd ed. Chicago, American Library Association, 1969.

School Media Quarterly. This journal is published four times a year by the American Association of School Librarians, a division of ALA. Subscriptions are available to AASL members and to libraries. Single copies may be purchased from ALA.

Bro-Dart Foundation, Box 306, Montoursville, Pennsylvania 17754.

The foundation published Virginia Gaver's *Elementary School Library Collection*, a large volume which lists, describes, evaluates and provides cataloging information for selected library books and audiovisual materials. This volume is revised each year to include new materials and remove outdated items.

Children's Book Council, Inc., 175 Fifth Avenue, New York, New York 10010.

Ask the council for their list of publications, and for information on available Book Week materials. You will want to see their pamphlet, *Planning a Book Fair*, if your school library is having such an event.

PUBLISHERS

R. R. Bowker Co., 1180 Avenue of the Americas, New York, New York 10036.

This firm publishes many books and aids for libraries; you will want to request their catalog. Two especially useful items are listed below.

Gillespie, John. *Introducing Books: A Guide for the Middle Grades.* New York, Bowker, 1970.

School Library Journal. This journal, published monthly from September to June, includes articles and book reviews. A related publication, *Previews*, is made up of reviews of audiovisual materials. SLJ is probably the most popular magazine for school librarians.

Educators Progress Service, Randolph, Wisconsin 53956.

This firm specializes in lists of free materials. These lists are updated annually. The one you will most probably want to purchase is *Elementary Teachers Guide to Free Curriculum Materials.*

Libraries Unlimited, Inc., P.O. Box 263, Littleton, Colorado 80120.

Write to this publishing house, specializing in books about library science and reference works, for their catalog.

Scarecrow Press, P.O. Box 656, Metuchen, New Jersey 08840.

Write for their catalog of publications on librarianship.

Superintendent of Documents, U.S. Government Printing Office, Washington, D.C. 20402.

Many inexpensive pamphlets are available from the federal government. Free price lists are available on a variety of different subjects including U.S. history, agriculture, homemaking, and many others. For additional information and descriptions of government publications to order, consult Linda Pohle's *A Guide to Popular Government Publications: For Libraries and Home Reference* (Littleton, Colo., Libraries Unlimited, Inc., 1972). You may write to the Superintendent of Documents and ask to be placed on the mailing list to receive free the *Selected U.S. Government Publications.* Issued periodically throughout the year, it describes new publications of popular interest and includes order forms.

H. W. Wilson Co., 950 University Avenue, Bronx, New York 10452.

Write for their catalog of library publications and indexing services. Two items of particular interest are listed below.

Children's Catalog. 12th ed. H. W. Wilson, 1971. This list of recommended children's library books includes descriptions and cataloging information.

The catalog is updated every six years or so, with annual supplements issued and provided as part of the purchase price until the next major revision.
Dewey, Melvil. *Abridged Dewey Decimal Classification and Relative Index.* Edition 10. Lake Placid Club, N.Y., Forest Press, 1971; distr. H. W. Wilson Co.
Sears List of Subject Headings. 10th ed. H. W. Wilson, 1972. This list of subject terms is the one most commonly used in cataloging school collections. It can also be used to set up a pamphlet file.

LIBRARY SUPPLY COMPANIES

Bro-Dart, 1609 Memorial Avenue, Williamsport, Pennsylvania 17701.

Write to this firm for a catalog of library supplies and services. They will also send you, free of charge, a booklet on mending books.

Demco, Box 1488, Madison, Wisconsin 53701.

Ask Demco for their catalog of library supplies and services. The firm also has available a pamphlet on book mending.

Gaylord Brothers, Inc., Syracuse, New York 13201.

Another firm dealing in library supplies—write for their catalog. Also request their free manual on book mending.

Highsmith Co., P.O. Box 25, Fort Atkinson, Wisconsin 53538.

Ask for their catalog of library supplies and equipment. A book mending pamphlet is also available.

BOOKS

In addition to the above materials from particularly helpful publishing houses and library sources, you may want to borrow or order the following books. Many of these have been mentioned throughout this book.

Arbuthnot, May Hill. *Children's Books Too Good to Miss.* 6th ed. Cleveland, Press of Case Western Reserve University, 1971.
Arbuthnot, May Hill. *Children's Reading in the Home.* Glenview, Ill., Scott Foresman, 1969.
Carter, Barbara, and Gloria Dapper. *School Volunteers: What They Do; How They Do It.* New York, Citation Press, 1972.
Gaver, Mary Virginia. *Effectiveness of Centralized Library Service in Elementary Schools.* New Brunswick, N.J., Rutgers University Press, 1963.

Larrick, Nancy. *Parents' Guide to Children's Reading.* Rev. ed. New York, Pocket Books, 1969.

Mott, Carolyn, and Leo B. Baisden. *The Children's Book on How to Use Books and Libraries.* 3rd ed. New York, Scribner's, 1968.

National Council of Teachers of English. *Adventuring with Books.* 2nd ed. New York, Citation Press, 1973.

Redl, Fritz. *When We Deal with Children.* New York, The Free Press, 1966.

Whitney, David C. *First Book of Facts and How to Find Them.* New York, Franklin Watts, 1966.

INDEX TO FILING RULES